# Road Cycling Manual

© Luke Edwardes-Evans 2016

First published in January 2017

British Library Cataloguing in Publication Data
A catalogue record for this book is available
from the British Library.

ISBN 978 1 78521 075 4

33614080154015

Library of Congress catalog card no. 2016937312

Published by Haynes Publishing,
Sparkford, Yeovil, Somerset BA22 7JJ, UK
Tel: 01963 440635
Int. tel: +44 1963 440635
Website: www.haynes.com

Haynes North America Inc.
859 Lawrence Drive, Newbury Park,
California 91320, USA

Printed and bound in Malaysia

| | |
|---|---|
| Author: | Luke Edwardes-Evans |
| Project Manager: | Louise McIntyre |
| Copy editor: | Ian Heath |
| Design: | James Robertson |
| Photography: | Time Inc (UK) Ltd Cycling Group, Andy Jones |
| Stock photos: | Shutterstock |

## Acknowledgements

Thanks to Time Inc (UK) Ltd Cycling Group/*Cycling Weekly* for photographs, and Dawn Brooks and Jason Hardy at Cycling Group for their help; to Andy Jones for selected photos; to Matt Levett for sourcing and compiling the images, with help from Niki Jones and Sarah Auld; and Christopher Catchpole and Daniel Gould for studio and riding images.

Special thanks to: Rebecca Charlton, Matt Levett and James Bracey for all their help and support; to my wife June for advice and encouragement; to Chris Sidwells for his support and comments; and to my unflappable editor, Louise McIntyre at Haynes.

# Road Cycling Manual

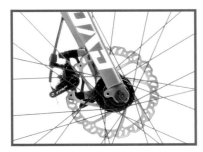

**THE ULTIMATE GUIDE TO PREPARING YOU AND YOUR BIKE FOR THE ROAD**

**Luke Edwardes-Evans**

# Contents

# Foreword

## by Sean Yates

*multiple British time trial champion and record holder, Tour de France stage-winner and yellow-jersey wearer, nine-time finisher of the Tour de France, and inductee of the British Cycling Hall of Fame*

When I started riding my bike around the Ashdown Forest in the 1970s, cycling was such a minority interest in the UK that it was barely considered a sport at all. Bike riders were viewed as faintly eccentric, oddly clothed and speaking in a lingo only understood by fellow clubmates. To the general public the sport of cycling was a lonely time-triallist, orange number attached with rusty safety pins, ploughing along a desolate dual-carriageway early on a Sunday morning.

I saw the other side of cycling when I went to live and race in France in the 1980s. On the Continent cycling was a hugely popular national sport, with rides and races for everyone from the keen amateur to famous professionals. My own 15-year career as a pro came to an end in 1996, but it was a few years after that before the success of British cyclists in the Olympic Games sparked a revolution in cycling that we could only have dreamed about 20 years ago.

Sporting success has propelled cycling into the news and made bike riding a pastime as popular and acceptable as running and swimming. Technology has also played a big part; bikes are lighter, more reliable, safer and faster than ever before and they look the absolute business. Carbon fibre, electronic gears and aerodynamics have transformed road bikes into awesome pieces of kit.

I didn't stop riding when I retired. I carried on racing as an amateur, mostly in time trials but I also did some sportives and enjoyed the freedom and fun of riding over a set distance without the pressure and hazards of a race. As a way to test yourself, an organised challenge ride with a signposted route and aid stations makes a lot of sense and I am not surprised sportives are so popular.

I may have stopped racing but my sons Liam and Jesse both race now, and I still love the buzz you get from bike racing. It's one of the hardest sports in the world and, for me, racing is still the truest test of cycling ability.

But whatever you choose to do on your bike, whether it's just a potter around your local roads or a race, as long as you never forget that feeling of excitement, freedom and adventure that we all had as kids on bikes, you'll forever be a cyclist.

**Sean Yates**

# Introduction

Riding a bicycle on the road is a great way to get fit. There are other ways to improve your fitness – like running, swimming and going to the gym – but none combine the low stresses that cycling puts on the body with the fun and fresh air kicks that you get every time you go out for a pedal. Because the bike is the most efficient machine ever devised, it can be ridden as slowly as you like with the absolute minimum of energy expenditure. Try that when you run or swim and you'll end up walking or sinking!

All you need to get fit is a bike and some comfortable clothing. There are bike-friendly paths in towns and parks where the novice rider can practise riding in a safe, traffic-free environment. Distance and time on the bike are completely up to you. Initially you might feel that 15 minutes is enough, but, because cycling is so enjoyable – addictive, even – you'll quickly want to stay out for longer and do more as your confidence grows.

Venturing further afield on to the open road opens up endless routes where the cyclist can ride for as long and as hard as he or she likes. Cycling is primarily an aerobic activity, greatly benefitting the heart, general circulation and all-round health. You'll get strong legs too, although it still pays to work on your core strength and upper body to balance-out your physique.

Cycling can be a pastime of extremes. A ride of a mile or two will provide health and fitness benefits, while at the other end of the scale there's almost no limit to how fit you can get from riding for hours, or sometimes days, on end. With your weight supported by the wheels and the zero impact of pedalling it's possible to put in marathon sessions, limited only by sleep deprivation. It's also possible to make huge efforts for extended periods of time, sometimes to exhaustion. If you want to burn thousands of calories, have incredible aerobic fitness and shapely legs, cycling is for you. It's no coincidence that some of the fittest athletes in the world are cyclists.

**Luke Edwardes-Evans**

# CHAPTER 1
# THE WORLD OF ROAD CYCLING

Where to start? Well, the great thing about road cycling is that it covers everything from the easiest, most relaxing ride imaginable to some of the most challenging physical and mental tests of any sport on the planet. From a tranquil pedal along peaceful country lanes to a multi-day long-distance race over iconic mountain passes, road cycling has got it all, and more. That's why road cycling is so popular; there are no conditions of entry – everyone is welcome.

It can be daunting, however, for the new cyclist to get a handle on the sheer volume of activities that road cycling offers. Not only that, the choice of bikes and kit seems to be endless; and although that's all part of the fun, it can also lead to expensive mistakes. Then there's the actual business of how, when and where to use much of the technical clothing and kit, some of which looks like nothing you've ever seen before!

← Hard riding is addictive and will get you incredibly fit.

And it doesn't take very long, especially if you start riding in groups, to realise that there's a lot more to cycling than thrusting on the pedals and keeping the bike in a straight line. Cycling is a sport of many skills and disciplines, with a lore of the road that's revered and handed down by an older generation of riders. It's fascinating, and it's all part of the addictive process of immersing yourself in the best sport in the world. To be a cyclist is a wonderful thing!

# Leisure cycling

Cycling is fun. You can ride a bike a long way and yet expend a minimum of effort. Pedalling gently along a flat road in an easy gear is one of the simplest pleasures of life. Coasting downhill requires no effort at all, unless you count the big grin on your face. And if the hill is too steep, who said you can't get off and walk up it?

Leisure cycling may not have the glamour of racing, the economic benefits of commuting or the fitness gains of sportives (see below), but it's a type of cycling that can bring a great deal of pleasure. As a way to get out in the fresh air with friends and family there's nothing better than a bike ride along quiet country lanes or cycle paths. Adults and children can potter along together, or couples can ride alongside each other chatting. It doesn't matter how far you go, a ride can be a few kilometres or take all of the day. All you need is a realistic destination, like a café or pub where you can treat yourself before the return trip.

Leisure cycling is becoming increasingly popular with older folk, who make use of cycle lanes and modern roadster bikes with comfortable riding positions and multiple gears. Machines with electric assist allow the rider to continue pedalling while an electric motor chips in with some additional help.

→ Cycling is a great way for families to enjoy a day out together.

# Cycling to work

Using a bicycle to get to and from work is the most popular use of the bike worldwide. Millions of people on bikes criss-cross towns and cities every day as they commute between work and home. Commuting by bike in today's traffic-choked towns makes a lot of sense, especially if you can avoid city-centre jams by silently bypassing them in bike lanes and along side streets.

Then there are the health benefits of daily exercise – which, incidentally, can be split equally between the physical and the cerebral – and finally the considerable financial savings of riding a bike set against public transport costs, running a vehicle and parking.

It's ironic that cycling used to be perceived as the transport option of folk who couldn't afford anything better. But now, when we look at Beijing, bikes are nowhere to be seen; the streets are clogged to a standstill by cars and smog, and we have to wonder where it all went wrong for the city famed the world over for its smoothly flowing rivers of bicycles.

Bikes can also be used for general transport; anything from visiting friends to going to the shops, or even for commercial use by couriers. Utility bikes with load bays and trailers can carry surprisingly bulky and heavy items that would defeat a small car.

➜ **Commuting to work on a bike brings fitness and cash benefits.**

# Cycle touring

Holidays on bikes – does it get much better than that? Touring on a bike is the ultimate two-wheeled escape. It matters not whether you disappear to the next parish for one night, cycling back home in time for tea the following day, or bid farewell to your loved ones and return a year later with tales of exotic places and exciting people. Touring can be as brief or drawn out as you like. The only thing you need is the spirit of adventure and some time off.

If you wish to be largely self-sufficient, camping is an option. You'll need to equip yourself and the bike, preferably with lightweight and compact kit all of which can otherwise result in a substantial payload. Many bikes can be adapted to carry luggage but some aren't up to the task, so you need to make sure your machine has strong enough wheels, provision for racks and powerful enough brakes before strapping your little world to its flanks.

Lightweight touring can be anything from a credit card in your back pocket, a superlight carbon road bike and a posh hotel programmed into the GPS, to a retro touring bike with saddlebag filled with espadrilles and hi-tech evening wear. Go with friends for laughs or go solo if you prefer to mull things over, but go touring – you'll love it.

← **Get away from it all on a touring holiday.**

# Cycle racing

Cycle racing on the road is a sport with a long and colourful history. Even during the very first days of the 'high', 'ordinary' or 'penny-farthing' bicycle in the late 1800s, the urge to compete inspired brave fellows to risk their necks – quite literally – in pursuit of the thrill and glory of winning. Races took place on the rough roads of the time, and later on metalled roads, often between big towns. Some of the oldest place-to-place road races in the calendar are well over a century old, testament to how embedded they've become in the sporting cultures of numerous regions around Europe.

Racing on the road flourished with the invention of the 'safety bicycle', and when the Tour de France rolled out of Paris early in the morning on 1 July 1904 cycling was already a well-established European sport, with mass appeal fomented by fantastic newspaper reports of the speed, bravery, endurance and chicanery of the new Kings of the Road.

Mass-start racing is the most traditional form of bike racing on the road. A bunch, or 'peloton', sets off together from one place towards another or around a set number of laps of a circuit. No matter how long the race or what the tactics are, the first rider across the line is the winner, simple as that.

Time trial competition is as old as road racing and pits the solo rider against a set distance, which is timed. Riders set off at regular intervals – usually one minute – and even if they catch and pass one another no 'drafting' is allowed. Every rider from first to last is given a time and a position in the field.

↑ Mass-start racing is the most popular branch of cycling competition.

## The Tour de France

More than any other cycle race the Tour de France has become an annual sporting phenomenon, drawing a global television audience of 3.5 billion, with 12 million roadside fans. The three-week race covers about 3,500km, mostly around France though often with early stages in adjacent countries. In 2016 the race started in Holland and in 2014 the Grande Depart drew massive crowds in Yorkshire and London.

→ Huge crowds turned out to cheer the Tour de France when it came to Yorkshire in 2014.

# Sportives and challenge rides

Sportives, also known as 'gran fondos', are the fastest-growing branch of cycle sport. Although not strictly a race, a sportive is individually timed and usually takes place on open roads with marshals or direction arrows. Distances can be from 50 to 250km, often with multiple ride options on the day. There's a trend towards longer events that are a challenging test of endurance as well as average speed. Closed-road sportives are rare but popular, and can attract fields in the tens of thousands.

Many new converts to cycling are drawn to sportives as they offer a similar challenge to running a marathon. A few months' serious training is required for anything over 100km, while the clothing and bikes can be high-tech but affordable. Cyclists set off in groups but can ride solo or in bunches. Many prefer to ride alone or move between groups. A timing chip records each rider's time, which can usually be accessed online after the event.

Some sportives are based on the great one-day classics and stage races. The daddy of them all is the Étape du Tour, which is an annual closed-road sportive along one of the mountain stages of the Tour de France. It's usually a sell-out, with more than 10,000 entrants. There are other legendary sportives across Europe and increasingly in the UK and USA.

← Sportive and challenge rides have introduced competitive cycling to thousands of new riders.

→ The Étape du Tour sportive follows a stage of the Tour de France on completely closed roads.

## Why you should enter a sportive

- You'll have a great day out on signposted scenic roads with food stops.
- You can ride with other cyclists or solo – it's up to you.
- You can challenge yourself to set a target time or average speed.
- There are no losers – everyone who finishes gets a medal and a time.
- If you have a problem there's usually technical and medical support.
- They're a chance to ride in another region or abroad.

→ Everyone's a winner in a sportive!

# Road cycling culture

A sport with nearly a century and a half of backstory comes with a lot of culture, a ton of baggage and a heap of mystique. This can be off-putting to someone considering cycling for the first time, and it can be baffling to new riders too. From the outside, road cycling is a pastime loaded with correct ways to dress and specific ways to conduct yourself on the road.

Take acknowledging other riders, for instance. This is something that drives traditional cyclists up the wall. They nod or wave to other bike riders and expect something in return. But how does the new rider know what to do if they're just riding along minding their own business?

Learning the etiquette of such matters was something that was passed down from old to new club cyclists in the days when just about every serious road cyclist had to join their local club before they were introduced to the lore of the road. Mostly this would happen just by watching how the more experienced riders conducted themselves. Now and again some instruction would be passed on, often in plain-speaking terms if a young rider did something rash on a club run. You soon learned not to do it again, especially when the advice came from a rider the same age as your dad.

Today's bike rider is more often than not an adult who may not take kindly to being torn off a strip by a grumpy bloke from the old school of cycling. Modern clubs have friendlier ways of passing on

a great deal of invaluable help and advice, with more experienced riders mentoring newcomers and rides organised for less confident cyclists. There's also an infinite amount of information in books, magazines and on the Internet.

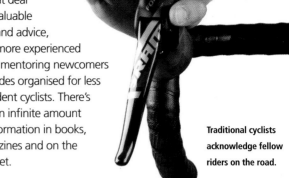

Traditional cyclists acknowledge fellow riders on the road.

## Six old-school cycling rules

- Always try to acknowledge another rider.
- Offer to help a cyclist stranded by the roadside.
- Ride side-by-side, not just in front of a ride buddy ('half-wheeling').
- Serious cyclists, especially racers, shave their legs.
- Your winter bike should be fitted with mudguards.
- It's uncool to go for Strava segments (see page 21) on a group ride.

# Joining a club

One of the best ways to progress as a cyclist is to join a club. Cycling may not be a team sport like football, for example, but club cycling is the rock on which the sport of cycling is built.

Joining a cycling club opens up a whole new world of friendships, experiences and knowledge. And if you want to compete, you're obliged to join a club, or at the very least the national federation.

From sportives to time trials or road racing, being in a club makes the whole process of becoming a cyclist easier and a lot more fun. There'll be others to help you decide what to enter, how to get there and what to do on the day. Above all there will be clubmates to ride with on weekend rides, training sessions and events.

Being in a cycling club gives the solo rider a sense of belonging. There's nothing wrong with the unattached bike rider, but being in a club is an acknowledgement that you're one of many fellow-minded souls, all sharing the joys of pedalling. Cycling can be hard and hazardous, so at times it's good to know that there are others out there ready to help and support you.

It's easy to join a club. There'll be one local to you, either named after the nearest town or something cycling-related, and usually followed by either CC (Cycling Club), Wheelers, RC (Road

← A club is the best way to get into bike racing at the grass roots.

→ British Cycling is behind many gold medals at world and Olympic level.

Club) or VC (Velo Club). Most clubs have their own websites or can be tracked down from the national federation list of clubs. Annual membership costs little more than the price of a sportive event, and beyond that there are few restrictive rules or regulations. All that every club needs in order to survive is enough volunteers to keep the club and its events going.

## British Cycling and Cycling UK

Two of the UK's biggest cycling organisations, either of these is worth joining for a range of benefits ranging from third-party insurance to a racing licence. British Cycling (BC) is the national federation representing cycling in the UK. It's primarily concerned with regulating racing in the UK, from grass roots through to the Olympics.

Cycling UK, formerly the Cyclists' Touring Club (CTC), is the UK charity for leisure cycling and has historically been a nationwide club for touring cyclists. In recent times it's broadened its appeal to encompass all types of leisure and fitness for riders of all ages. It also operates a very effective political lobby group on behalf of cycling. Cycling UK is one of the oldest cycling clubs in the world. It was founded in 1878 and was originally called the Bicycle Touring Club.

If you want to race, you almost certainly need to join your national federation and then take out a racing licence through them. For most organised cycling events there's a requirement for third-party insurance, and the licence in part covers that. It will also allow you to train as a coach or become a race organiser or official. Membership of BC and Cycling UK also gives you access to services, special offers and deals.

Cycling UK has traditionally operated very effectively on a local level, with District Associations organising regular club rides that are a great way for individual members to meet up for sociable rides. In more recent times British Cycling has also had

considerable success with its mass-participation BC Sky Rides on closed city-centre circuits, and also with Breeze rides aimed at encouraging more women into cycling.

↓ Women-only rides have introduced the sport to a new generation of female cyclists.

# Solo versus group riding

Both are great! Most riders start cycling on their own, and setting off with that exciting feeling of slight apprehension laced with the spirit of adventure never leaves you. Riding solo is easy. Leave when you like, go anywhere at any speed and roam to your heart's content.

Training rides, when you need to vary your pace or practise certain skills, can only be done on your own. It could be hill reps or intervals, cornering practice or sprint training, many types of structured riding are best done alone. Even unstructured training – when the aim might be to attack every hill, for instance – can be irksome for the other rider, not to say rather anti-social.

You may enjoy solo riding for the simplest of reasons. Cycling along lost in thought, freed from the ties of everyday concerns, is one of life's solitary pleasures and it's why many folk prefer to pedal alone. Fast or slow, long or short, it doesn't matter, there's no stigma in riding alone. It doesn't have to be an existential exercise either – pushing yourself and enjoying the sensations of working hard and concentrating on a single activity can be extremely satisfying. On busy or narrow roads it can also be a lot less stressful to ride solo than in a group that's possibly holding up traffic or riding in a style that doesn't suit your own.

Group cycling is a complete contrast to riding solo. Riding two-abreast or in a tight group it's quite possible to talk comfortably to an adjacent rider. Indeed, cycling is one of the few athletic sports where this is possible. Running and chatting isn't nearly so easy! Incidentally, cycling is also the only sport in which one participant can physically help another, by placing a hand

↑ Serious training sessions like hill reps are best done on your own.

on their back to transfer some energy. A strong cyclist can push another one home if, for instance, their chain breaks.

Cycling in a group is a discipline that takes practice and some nerve. Placing your bike close to the one in front and within elbow-touching distance of a rider alongside is a skill that's well worth learning. There's nothing like bowling along in a fast-moving bunch of cyclists – it's one of the most exciting and fun things you can do on a bike.

↓ Riding alone is one of the most appealing solitary pleasures of cycling.

# Personal liability and cycle insurance

It's well worth insuring your bike or bikes, especially if you have to leave them outside now and again. Commuting by bike is when you're most likely to have your bike stolen, as it'll often be locked up outside. Most household insurance policies cover bikes up to a certain level, but check the policy in detail for the values covered and the terms relating to a claim away from your property.

Many insurance companies offer policies specifically aimed at cyclists and you may find the best deals through membership of a national cycling organisation like British Cycling or Cycling UK. For personal liability cover, either for racing or general riding, by far the best solution is to join one of the big cycling organisations, which offer third-party cover as part of their membership package.

↑ It's worth insuring your bike, especially if you ride to work or around town.

# Online communities

There's a massive global community of cyclists out there and many of them are a swipe away on your smartphone. It's never been easier to connect with other cyclists, via the Internet, cycling apps and even through online lonely hearts columns! Cycling computers can now be used to map rides, record segments and provide a raft of physiological data from heart rate to power output. Everything can then be downloaded automatically to your computer at home. Your friends or fellow app users can share and compare routes, segment times and physical data.

Strava is one of the most popular cycling applications worldwide. Free to download to a smartphone or cycling computer with GPS, Strava records your ride with distance, average speeds and total elevation. It also records segments of your route, which are ranked against the same segments ridden by other riders. The fastest rider along each segment is number one and there can be thousands of riders ranked in some segments. Just about every stretch of road in every cycling region is chopped into segments, but there's nothing to stop you creating your own segment and uploading it to Strava.

Other, less performance-based apps bring together cyclists wishing to share their favourite routes with others. These online communities are in effect loosely based clubs and there's nothing to stop them meeting up for rides or sharing their experiences online. Even Twitter has proved to be a potent means of communication among cyclists, with hundreds turning up for pop-up club runs with celebrity cyclists, while also vociferously countering anti-cycling comments.

Cycling clubs will invariably have their own website and probably a Facebook page. In the Internet age it's hard to be a cyclist and not be a small part of the online global cycling community.

⬇ Strava is one of the most popular bike-riding apps.

## Twelve popular cycling apps

- Strava – records rides with segment times.
- Zwift – turbo training virtual racer.
- MapMyRide – route plotter and resource.
- Fill That Hole – UK app for reporting potholes.
- Size My Bike – handy bike-sizing tool.
- Cyclemeter – routes and training.
- CycleMaps – cycle routes mapping tool.
- Endomondo – virtual coach with training drills.
- Kinomap Trainer – turbo training tool with video.
- Garmin Connect – connects GPS to your mobile.
- Bike Gear Calculator – matches cadence and speed to your gear.
- CycleMaps – cycle route planner using safe streets.

# CHAPTER 2
# BUYING A BIKE

There's never been a better time to buy a bike. Modern materials and construction standards are at an all-time high. Best of all, the trickle-down effect of some of the best innovations in recent times means that even entry-level machines can benefit from functions seen on pro team bikes from a year or two ago.

Gone, too, are the days when the only way to acquire a quality road bike involved sourcing a hand-built frame of your choice, then buying the components before having them 'built up' into a complete machine. Oh, and you probably had to have the wheels assembled by hand too, after agreeing with the wheel builder which spokes, hubs and rims to use.

Most new bikes come as complete machines, with the big brands offering every combination of frame and groupset from starter road bikes to models that are identical to a professional team bike used in the Tour de France. They can, in fact, be lighter, because the world governing body's weigh limit of 15lb (6.8kg) doesn't apply to bikes for non-professional riders.

→ A carbon fibre road bike is an ultra-lightweight thing of beauty.

# Bike shops

Buying a bike should be fun and it is, especially if it's from a good bike shop. There's nothing quite like walking into a well-stocked showroom and feasting your eyes on rows of new machines all vying for your attention. Extract a bike from the display, sit on it, hold the bars, and you really get a feel for that particular machine. Lift it up and feel how light it is, try the brake levers for reach and the saddle for comfort. You'll know in short order whether to consider buying that model or size of bike or to look for something else.

In a good bike shop there'll be an attentive sales assistant, who should have established what type of cycling you like and what you'd like to achieve by buying a new bike. This may involve some open-ended questions and should presume nothing about your aims or ability. A friendly interrogation from the sales person isn't as easy as it sounds, as they're trying to identify your new bike, which should, of course, suit your current level of cycling.

⬇ **A good bike shop is an Aladdin's Cave of tasty machines and accessories.**

A thoughtful sales assistant will also offer you a machine capable of satisfying not just your short-term goals, but more ambitious ones too. Get the right bike and one thing is guaranteed – you'll want to ride more than ever before.

Most towns have at least one bike shop and the standard these days is much higher than it used to be, when bike shops had a reputation for brusque service and gnomic jargon. A franchised dealer with one of the big brands should have a bright and welcoming showroom with knowledgeable staff trained to help you through the buying process.

There's quite a lot more to it than simply selecting the machine and size, and that's where the bike shop can really help, with advice on the fit of various elements of the bike ranging from saddle height to stem length and even crank length. A good bike shop will swap out components like stems and even saddles if they don't suit you. There may be some negotiation involved, but it's far better to walk out of the shop with a bike that fits perfectly than waste time and money putting things right later.

# Online shopping

Ordering a bike online has never been easier and the Internet's ruthless facility to hunt down the best deals makes it an irresistible tool for many cyclists. Buying a bike online can be done from the website belonging to a sole trader or shop, or from one of the big players offering a bewildering array of brands and deals. Many sites have sizing and configuration options and if you know exactly what you want, from frame size to stem length and maybe even crank length, you can order the perfect bike for you after a single session on the computer.

Configuring a bike involves various levels of specifying individual components based on price, size or preference. It's possible to buy the frame and then pick various build options from groupsets through to the wheels, but most bikes come with everything apart from pedals and your choice will have to be based on simply model and size. And that's fine for most people, as there'll often be a size that comes very close to their requirements.

However, the downside of ordering a complete bike on the Internet is that you risk making a potentially costly mistake, because you haven't figured out what you really want or how well

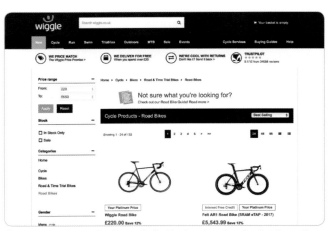

↑ It helps to know exactly what you're looking for when shopping for bikes online.

the bike will fit you. Even experienced cyclists can do with some help and advice from a third party now and again, and that's when the Internet falls short of what a good bike shop can offer.

# The best bike for you

There are hundreds of bikes to choose from and it's all too easy to make a mistake if you're new to cycling or not one for poring over the technical pros and cons of every component. If road cycling is the primary objective, that helps a lot, as you can ignore mountain bikes with unnecessary suspension, additional weight and sluggish wheels and tyres.

However, a hybrid machine – which is similar to a mountain bike but with standard road-bike wheels and without the weighty suspension forks or back end – can be a versatile and forgiving introduction to road cycling. Hybrids with aluminium frames are affordable and generally considered to be a sensible entry-level machine for introductory fitness riding, traffic-free paths, commuting and touring. At the other end of the scale are top-end hybrid road bikes made from carbon fibre and equipped with the best components and electronic gears.

Side by side, the affordable hybrid and the expensive road rocket have very little in common. Your choice of bike will very likely fall midway between both machines,

hopefully combining the best elements of versatility, affordability and performance into the ideal package.

← A versatile hybrid bike has flat bars with road wheels and multiple MTB-type gears.

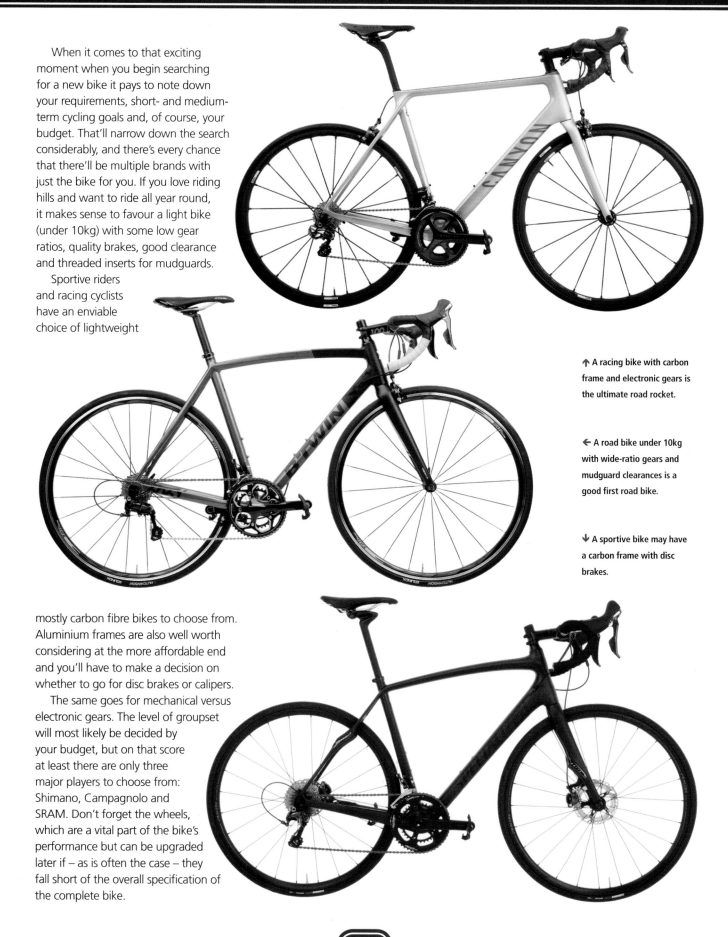

When it comes to that exciting moment when you begin searching for a new bike it pays to note down your requirements, short- and medium-term cycling goals and, of course, your budget. That'll narrow down the search considerably, and there's every chance that there'll be multiple brands with just the bike for you. If you love riding hills and want to ride all year round, it makes sense to favour a light bike (under 10kg) with some low gear ratios, quality brakes, good clearance and threaded inserts for mudguards.

Sportive riders and racing cyclists have an enviable choice of lightweight

↑ A racing bike with carbon frame and electronic gears is the ultimate road rocket.

← A road bike under 10kg with wide-ratio gears and mudguard clearances is a good first road bike.

↓ A sportive bike may have a carbon frame with disc brakes.

mostly carbon fibre bikes to choose from. Aluminium frames are also well worth considering at the more affordable end and you'll have to make a decision on whether to go for disc brakes or calipers.

The same goes for mechanical versus electronic gears. The level of groupset will most likely be decided by your budget, but on that score at least there are only three major players to choose from: Shimano, Campagnolo and SRAM. Don't forget the wheels, which are a vital part of the bike's performance but can be upgraded later if – as is often the case – they fall short of the overall specification of the complete bike.

# Ensuring the bike fits

No matter how expensive the bike, if it's the wrong size or incorrectly fitted, it'll never feel right and could seriously affect your enjoyment of cycling. In extreme cases a badly fitted bike can lead to aches and pains and, eventually, long-term injury. But that's the worst-case scenario – many cyclists ride for years quite happily and relatively comfortably on slightly ill-fitting bikes. If only they knew how much more enjoyable, efficient and cosseting a correctly sized and fitted bike can be!

At one time the only fitting advice you might get from a

shop was the frame size, and even that could be a hit-and-miss affair with often only half a dozen frame sizes based solely on the length of the seat tube. If your body shape fell outside of the median you could well end up with a bike that fitted in one direction but not the other. Changing stems and handlebars took guesswork plus rides down high streets where you could look at your reflection in plate glass shop windows.

These days there's no need to go to such hazardous lengths, as most bike shops offer a bike-fitting service that takes the risk out of choosing a wrong-size bike. There's a cost involved, but some shops will factor this into the price of a new bike, and once you have your baseline dimensions you can use them for years thereafter. Not only will you now know your ideal frame size, but a bike-fitting session will also determine saddle height, reach to the bars, crank length and knee position over the pedals. Your preferred type of drop handlebar – its width, shape and depth – is also a very useful piece of information to carry over to future machines.

← A professional bike fitter will ascertain crucial things like saddle height and hip angle.

↓ Many bike shops offer bike-fitting services that they can factor into the price of a new bike.

# Buying new

A new bike can offer exceptional value. Add up the sum of its parts and invariably the total will be significantly higher than the ticket price. Most big-brand bike manufacturers use their buying power to do deals on groupsets and wheels that are impossible to match if you were to buy the frame then purchase the individual components. Internet retailers and online-only bike brands can do astounding deals on bikes, charging roughly the price of the frame and virtually chucking in the rest for free.

Price aside, a new bike is always worth considering because, unlike a car, bicycles are quite fragile things that can be easily marked, damaged or worn out. Buying new takes the risk out of putting right a used bike with worn-out parts. On a used

↑ **Internet-only bike brands can offer unrivalled deals on complete bikes.**

bike not only could you be in for repairs or costly replacement of consumables but there'll also be no opportunity to select individual parts for preference or fit.

There's nothing like the feel of a new bike. Everything feels smooth and well screwed together. The cables are whip tight and the brakes are full of feel and power. The pristine chain slots seamlessly between shiny silver sprockets on the cassette and the chainset is unmarked. All you want to do is look at your perfect new friend, which may even be allowed into the front room for those few precious days before the first ride.

# Buying second-hand

There are bargains to be had in the used bike market but it pays to go in with eyes wide open and a healthy dose of scepticism. Inevitably there's a thriving black market in stolen bikes and components, so before making any purchasing decisions you should be confident that you're dealing with a genuine seller. If it doesn't feel right, walk away. Nearly new individual components, complete bicycles and frames are all potentially suspect, whereas items like shoes or clothing are less likely to be stolen.

Antenna fully extended, the search for used bike parts can be an absorbing and fun pastime. The Internet has opened up the market for second-hand bicycles, parts and accessories massively, and many hours can be wiled away searching for the exact item on your wish list.

Auction websites are the most popular places to look, but there are two pitfalls to avoid. The first is paying too much in the heat of the moment, or as the clock counts down to the end of the bidding process. As a general rule you should aim to pay around half of the original retail price of the item on which you're bidding, and if it creeps above that have a maximum and stick to it. It's surprising what some people will pay for something they haven't seen or that they could buy for much less with a little more patience and hunting.

The second pitfall is buying something that you haven't seen and inspected. With some components, like brake calipers for instance, it's possible to tell the condition of the item from a good-quality image. There isn't much that can be damaged or go wrong with a set of brakes, or items like seatposts, saddles, front derailleurs and stems. But there are lots of components that could easily be damaged or bent in a way that may not show up in pictures. Top of the list are frames and wheels. Don't buy a used bicycle frame without inspecting it in person, either before you make an offer or after you've bid on the proviso that the frame passes muster on collection.

A frame or forks can be bent in a crash, or could have a dent or even a crack. The dropouts could be bent and threaded inserts from the bottle cage mounts to the bottom bracket could be stripped. Wheels are the other fragile, expensive items, which should be carefully checked either before buying or at the very least on collection.

Building a bike from the frame up with second-hand components is something you should only do if you have the knowledge and experience of working on bikes. It takes a trained

← The only way to check if a frame is damaged or has been repaired is to inspect it in person.

➔ A cared-for used bike is well worth considering if you budget for a good service.

eye to determine how much wear is left in a drivetrain or whether a frame is a few millimetres out of track. Even on parts with plenty of life left in them there can be additional costs for consumables like brake pads or chains, which can eat away at budgets.

But if you're looking to create a unique machine, or for parts which can't be obtained, buying second-hand is the only way to go; and even if you make some mistakes along the way, buying used can be a very enjoyable and affordable way to get a bike.

## Building your own bike

Not that long ago the only way to acquire a quality road bike involved buying a frame and then building it up with parts selected by you. You'd have had to get the wheels built by hand too, by a specialist wheel builder.

From ordering a frame to delivery of a complete bike could take weeks, or even months if it was a hand-built steel frame from a reputable builder. The waiting was torture, but the day of arrival was one of pure joy. There are no shortcuts if you

want a hand-built steel or titanium frame, and if you can find a wheel builder you too can enjoy the agony and the ecstasy of the 1980s lightweight bike customer.

Building a bike from the frame up may seem like an odd thing to do. You wouldn't buy an engine and then hunt around for seats and cupholders and the like if you were buying a car, and that indeed is the reaction of most folk, who are quite happy to buy a complete bike. But the wonderful thing about a bike is that it's composed of a couple of dozen key components, not hundreds as is the case for a car or motorcycle.

↓ It can be very satisfying to put together the individual components of a bike

# Types of bike

## Hybrid

Ideal starter bike for the novice rider, a hybrid is basically a roadgoing mountain bike with powerful easy-to-reach brakes, and an upright riding position with wide flat handlebars offering lots of control. Having no suspension keeps the weight down, but the fat, rugged tyres can be run at comfortably low pressures to compensate.

### → Best for

Commuting, short leisure rides, gravel paths, sedate touring.

### → Key features

Flat handlebars, aluminium or carbon frame with 700c wheels and tough tyres, disc brakes, rack and mudguard mounts. Triple chainset with wide range of gears.

### → Shall I get one?

If you want a versatile and user-friendly bike for general riding or commuting to work, a hybrid can meet all your needs. For longer or faster riding a hybrid can't compete with a lighter machine with a sportier riding position and drop handlebars

Wide ratio cassette with seven to 11 sprockets from 11 to 34 teeth.

Comfortable saddle with more padding than a racing model.

Rear derailleur with long jockey arm to cope with wide-ratio cassette.

Triple chainset but may also have a compact twin-ring chainset. Latest models could be fitted with single ring chainset and 11-speed cassette.

Sloping top tube allows more stand-over room with fewer sizing options. Hybrid frames mostly aluminium (pictured) but top-end models made from carbon fibre and titanium.

Flat bars with rubber grips. Brake and gear levers within easy reach. Riding position is usually more upright with fewer hand positions than a drop handlebar.

Caliper brakes are either cantilever or V-brake type. Both allow the fitment of a wide range of tyres. Many hybrids are equipped with disc brakes, either cable or hydraulically operated.

Flat pedals without clips or a quick-release system are common on hybrids, especially if the bike is used for short rides or family cycling. For longer rides a mountain bike double-sided quick-release pedal like Shimano SPD is recommended.

Rigid fork keeps the weight down and helps the hybrid handle like a road bike. Some hybrids have a suspension fork which adds weight and is only effective on very bumpy terrain.

Wheels are 700c, the same as a standard road bike. Wider rim allows fitment of a wide range of tyres from slick road to MTB knobblies.

# Touring

Traditional machine with drop handlebars, mudguards, rack, panniers and stronger wheels than a sports bike. Ideal for longer rides with overnight stays or even camping. The frame is usually steel and built for comfort and stability when loaded up.

### ➜ Best for
Weekends away or longer touring holidays, but can be stripped down for winter training and commuting too.

### ➜ Key features
Drop handlebars, steel frame (often hand-built) with rack mounts front and rear and mudguards. Compact gearing with 32- or 36-spoke wheels.

### ➜ Shall I get one?
Absolutely! A hand-built touring bike or even an off-the-peg machine is your ticket to short breaks with friends or longer holidays further afield and some of the best times you can have on two wheels.

Traditional leather saddle, once broken in, can be more comfortable than racing models on long rides. Comes with eyelets for attaching a saddle bag.

Mudguards on a touring bike keep water and dirt off the machine and rider. They also protect saddlebags and panniers from soaking spray.

A wide-ratio cassette is best and most touring bikes will come with at least nine speeds at the back. The rear derailleur should have a long jockey arm to handle sprockets bigger than 28 teeth.

Any frame material can be used for a touring bike but steel (pictured) and titanium lend themselves to custom builds, with exact sizing and accessories specified by the rider.

Drop handlebars are well suited for long rides on a touring bike as they offer multiple riding positions. Bars may be set higher than on a sportive or race bike with brake levers also further up the bars.

Standard 700c road wheels are popular on touring bikes and can be lightweight for fast touring or more heavily built for load carrying. Winter road tyres or four-season versions are best suited for most touring.

A touring frame should have threaded inserts for two bottle cages and for the fitment of a rack on the rear seat stays. Custom frames may also be fitted with a pump peg under the top tube, rack mounts on the front forks or spare spoke carrier on the rear stays.

Chainset will most likely be compact but triples (pictured) are also popular for touring and there is nothing wrong with mid-compact or racing if a wide ratio 10 or 11 speed cassette is used.

Steel fork has generous amount of rake to soak up vibrations and offer relaxed handling. Comes with threaded inserts for fitment of front rack.

Disc brakes are increasingly popular on touring bikes as they allow the fitment of fatter, heavy duty tyres and are more effective than traditional caliper or cantilever brakes on a heavily laden machine.

Cassette on a sportive bike should be at least eight speeds and on quality models will be 10 or 11.

Lightweight but comfortable saddle ideal for long rides. Carbon or titanium frame rails shed a few grams and offer a modicum of damping.

Carbon frame designed to allow more comfort-damping than a pure race bike. Thinner seat stays and more flexible seat tube or post are popular solutions.

Top-end derailleurs perform faultlessly and can be cable or electrically operated.

Chainset can be compact, mid-compact or standard racing offering the biggest gears. Most riding, especially on hilly courses, can easily be ridden using a compact chainset with a 10 or 11-speed wide-ratio cassette.

Clip-in road pedals are one-sided and designed for use with a rigid soled road shoe.

Compact handlebars are popular on sportive bikes as they make it easier to hold a tuck position while on the drops.

A longer head tube is popular on sportive bikes as it raises the front end offering a more upright riding position for riders less inclined to adopt a racing tuck position.

## Sportive

A quality road bike capable of long road rides in relative comfort and at a fair pace. Can be a versatile machine, with disc brakes and mountings for mudguards making it suitable for training, commuting and even entry-level racing.

### ➜ Best for
Sportives of 60km to 200km, fast training, fitness riding, varied terrain including long hills. Commuting in the summer months and can even be raced or used for triathlon.

### ➜ Key features
Carbon frame with tall head tube and higher handlebars. Back end designed to absorb road vibrations, either with damped couplings or 'tuned' seat and chain stays. Weighs less than 9kg and looks like a race bike.

### ➜ Shall I get one?
If you like sports and fitness cycling, with sportives and long rides your main objectives, a sportive bike makes perfect sense, especially if you prefer a more upright position and lower gears for the hills.

Disc brakes are increasingly popular on sportive bikes as they offer powerful braking in all conditions. They also permit the use of lightweight oversize tyres due to generous clearances and the absence of caliper brakes.

Lightweight wheels with aero rims made from alloy or carbon are ideal for sportives. Wider rims allow fitment of quality road tyres larger than 25c which can be run at lower pressures with no trade-off in rolling resistance.

E-gear connector wire is only visible cable as all the wiring is routed through the frame for maximum aero advantage.

Lightweight minimalist racing saddle has carbon rails and sits on a carbon aero seat post offering a few centimetres of adjustment.

Carbon fibre road frame features the most radical aerodynamic tube profiles permissible within the rules of the world governing body.

Shimano Dura-Ace Di2 was the first E-gear system with mass appeal and it has proved its reliability on multiple Tour de France winning bikes.

Racing chainset has hollow crank arms and chainrings to reduce weight and maximise rigidity.

Aerodynamic downtube is similar to a TT bike – even the bottle cage mounts are flush with the trailing edge.

Designed to be an integral fit to the front end with Aheadset spacers and bearing cups shaped to reduce turbulence behind the handlebars.

Flaps in head tube open when wheel is turned to allow hidden brake cable to operate the caliper.

## Race

Road bike built for speed and little else. As light as possible, designed to offer the most aerodynamic riding position and with few concessions to comfort.

### ➜ Key features

Carbon frame honed in a wind tunnel, lightweight deep-section carbon wheels with high-quality lightweight tyres. Bigger, non-compact chainrings with electronic or superlight derailleurs. Lively, very responsive handling.

### ➜ Best for

Winning! A race bike is the quickest type of road bike, so if you want to fly along on your own, beat your mates to the town sign or compete in mass-start road events, you need a race bike.

### ➜ Shall I get one?

Even if you only ride a race bike on sunny days and on smooth roads, there's nothing to match the buzz of owning a badass competition bike. From its looks to the sheer exhilaration of the ride it's worth every penny.

Straight carbon fork with aero blades is shaped to fit the frame most notably at the top where the crown is designed for a flush fit with the head tube and front brake.

Carbon rims with wide track can take fatter, modern racing tyres of 25c and above.

# Time trial

Time trialling is a solo timed event normally held under club cycling rules or as part of a triathlon. A time trial bike is one of the most specialist bikes you can buy, and not suitable for anything other than time trial training and racing.

### → Key features

Set up for an aero tuck riding position using ultra narrow bars. Carbon frame and components designed to cut through the air with minimal turbulence. Wheels have very deep rims and often a disc rear. High gears.

### → Best for

Time trialling over set distances or circuits, usually from ten to a hundred miles. Solo and unpaced, the idea is to go as fast as possible, and the winner is the one with the quickest time.

### → Shall I get one?

Only if you want to race time trials or are a serious triathlete.

Time trial saddles can be angled down to rotate the rider into a more aero position. They may also have a shorter nose to comply with UCI regulations concerning the position of the saddle in relation to the bottom bracket.

Rear wheel with deep carbon rim, aerodynamic or flat spokes and tyre which fits snugly against the rim and seat tube fairing. A full disc wheel can also be used in the rear.

Electronic rear derailleur ensures faultless cog swaps with no more than a button push while the rider maintains an aero tuck on the bars.

Chainset with a big ring with at least 53 teeth. Solid chainring more aerodynamic and stiff.

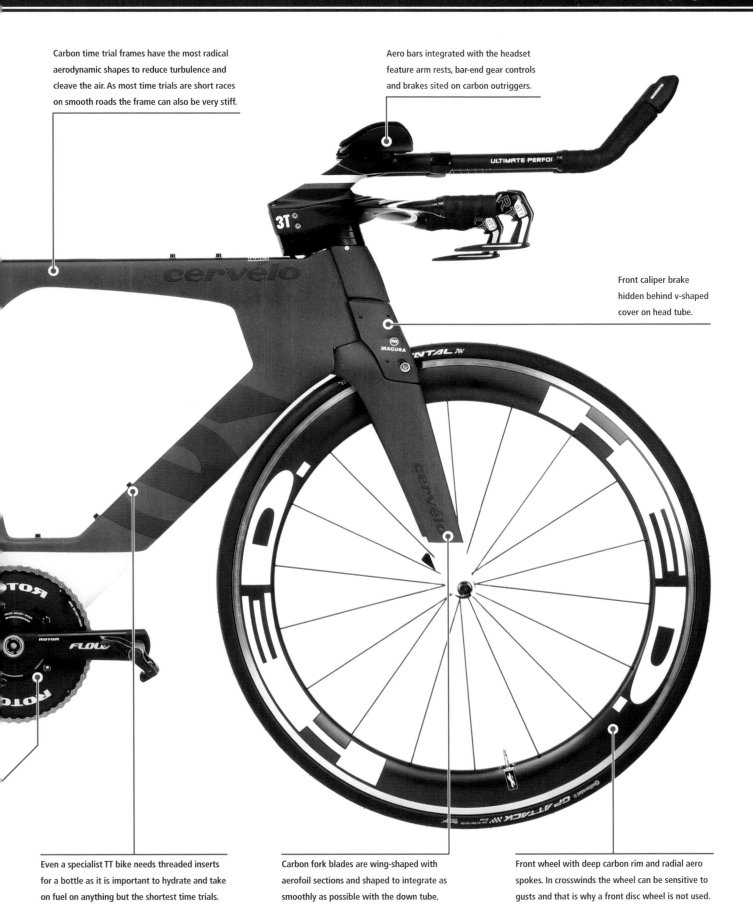

Carbon time trial frames have the most radical aerodynamic shapes to reduce turbulence and cleave the air. As most time trials are short races on smooth roads the frame can also be very stiff.

Aero bars integrated with the headset feature arm rests, bar-end gear controls and brakes sited on carbon outriggers.

Front caliper brake hidden behind v-shaped cover on head tube.

Even a specialist TT bike needs threaded inserts for a bottle as it is important to hydrate and take on fuel on anything but the shortest time trials.

Carbon fork blades are wing-shaped with aerofoil sections and shaped to integrate as smoothly as possible with the down tube.

Front wheel with deep carbon rim and radial aero spokes. In crosswinds the wheel can be sensitive to gusts and that is why a front disc wheel is not used.

Wide-ratio cassette with 10 or 11 speeds with at least a 32-tooth bottom sprocket.

Comfortable saddle suited to on and off-road use with more padding than a racing saddle.

Carbon frame is light and designed to offer some flex over rough terrain. High front end for an upright riding position and easier command of the bars and controls.

Rear derailleur with long jockey arm can cope with wide-ratio cassette. Most gravel bikes are fitted with mechanical gears.

Chainset most likely to be compact with twin chainrings but single-ring options are also increasingly popular when teamed with an 11-speed cassette.

Road pedals can be used if the bike is mostly used on the road, but for mixed use twin-sided MTB pedals and shoes are more versatile.

Unlike a hybrid, which is similar in other respects, a gravel bike has drop handlebars offering a wide range of riding positions on and off road.

Forks and back end have generous clearances designed to offer a stable and comfortable ride.

## Gravel-cross

Not a cyclo-cross race bike but a versatile all-rounder with frame, clearances, tyres and disc brakes suitable for road riding as well as off-road on unpaved or gravel trails. Specialist cyclo-cross bikes are intended only for off-road racing.

### ➔ Key features

Carbon frame with clearances for extra fat tyres and mud. Upright riding position with disc brakes and strong wheels. Similar weight to a sportive bike but not as light as a cyclo-cross race bike.

### ➔ Shall I get one?

It's a robust sportive bike with the versatility and toughness to ride seriously off-road. Good as an only bike for commuting and weekend rides on all terrain

Tyres from 28 to 40c can be fitted thanks to wider rims and generous clearances. Rider can choose between lightweight road tyres to serious off-road knobblies.

Gravel bikes have disc brakes which allow powerful braking in all conditions and wheels which can be fitted with a wide range of tyres.

# CHAPTER 3
# THE BIKE

'Simplify, then add lightness,' said Colin Chapman about his legendary Lotus racing cars that won races thanks to great handling, minimal weight and just the right amount of power. He could easily have been talking about bicycles, because those words mean as much to a cyclist as they do to a racing-car driver.

Less is more when it comes to road bikes – or 'racing' bikes, as they used to call anything with drop handlebars and derailleur gears. It implied that while there were many other types of machine, only one was worthy of the ultimate appellation 'racer'!

A road bike represents the pinnacle of design and material technology, which in recent times has reached hitherto undreamed of levels of lightness, strength and reliability. Racing cyclists have never had so many gears in such a light yet stiff and great-handling package. Tyres and braking systems offer astonishing levels of grip and stopping power. Aerodynamic wheels and frames cut through the air, saving seconds per mile.

And the best thing about a racing bike? You don't have to be a racer to own and enjoy one. For the price of a city car you could get a bike good enough to win the Tour de France. For a quarter of that you could have something that is almost as 'performant' and can be upgraded with extra lightness!

⬇ **The modern bicycle is an eclectic mix of the exotic and the traditional.**

# Frame materials and construction

## Steel

After wood, used for the first hobby horses and earliest forms of self-propelled transport at the turn of the 1800s, wrought iron and then steel were the materials of choice for the boneshakers, 'high ordinaries' or 'penny-farthings' when cycling took off in the mid to late nineteenth century. When the earliest iterations of the safety bike – the forerunner of today's road bicycle – began to appear in the 1880s steel was used for the diamond frame, the spokes and ancillary parts from rims to ball bearings.

For the next 100 years mainstream bicycles had diamond-shaped frames built with steel tubes brazed or welded together by hand. By the 1920s lightweight double-butted steel tubes using manganese steel alloy and advanced brazing techniques could produce a frame almost comparable in weight and ride quality to one produced today.

Ultra lightweight steel tubesets from Reynolds (UK), Columbus (Italy), Vitus (France) and True Temper (USA) pushed the limits of steel frames in the 1980s just when mass-produced aluminium and titanium frames began to match and then exceed steel in terms of performance, weight and price. Steel's decline from then on was rapid, and when carbon-fibre bikes became widely available in the 1990s the game was up for steel bike frames. But then, as the millennium came round, a new generation of artisan frame builders began a small but welcome revival of the handmade steel frame.

Steel has many devotees despite its weight disadvantage over a carbon frame. Its innate flexibility offers a smooth ride on rough roads and handling full of feedback and stability. Custom steel can be tailored to an individual's exact dimensions, as well as cater for specific requirements, from

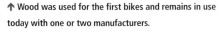

↑ Wood was used for the first bikes and remains in use today with one or two manufacturers.

↑ The steel 'diamond' frame hasn't changed radically in 100 years.

multiple mounting points to ornate lugwork. Most pleasingly a hand-built steel frame can be a creative work of art with unique combinations of paint, finish and artistry.

↓ Traditional steel frames are built by hand and can be tailored to fit.

→ A modern hand-built steel frame is a thing of great beauty and a joy to ride.

## Aluminium

There's very little that's new in cycling so you may not be surprised to know that aluminium was used to make parts for a bicycle as far back as the 1890s. Joining aluminium tubes took many decades to perfect, however, and it wasn't until the 1970s that aluminium tubes began to make an impact on lightweight road bikes.

Thick-gauge aluminium tubes were inserted into lugs and usually glued or pinned in place by frame makers ALAN (Italy) and Vitus (France). Later in the same decade welded aluminium frames from the USA used thinner gauge oversized tubes, and these framesets matched the best steel ones for weight and exceeded them in stiffness.

↑ Aluminium road bikes often use distinctive oversized tubes.

↑ Marco Pantani's Tour de France win in 1998 was the high point for aluminium racing bikes.

Until the late 1990s very light TIG-welded aluminium frames, many of them mass produced in Taiwan, became the default choice for road racing, their high point being Marco Pantani's victory at the 1998 Tour de France aboard an aluminium Bianchi. When Lance Armstrong won the Tour a year later he was on a carbon Trek, and from that day on aluminium fell from favour.

Aluminium is an excellent material for bikes as it's readily available and easy to work into tubes and components ranging from derailleurs to rims. Using thin-walled tubes can result in

↓ A lightweight aluminium road bike is hard to beat in terms of price and performance.

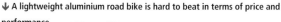

a very light frame, comparable in weight to high-end carbon fibre, and that explains why aluminium, though not found in the professional ranks any more, remains a savvy option for cyclists looking for a lightweight and affordable bike.

There's one downside to aluminium, which is its finite fatigue life. In order to reduce flex an aluminium frame has to be stiffer than frames built with more forgiving materials or lay-ups. That's why aluminium frames have a reputation for a hard ride and aren't always favoured by cyclists who rate comfort alongside performance. But on more compliant wheels shod with today's bigger volume road tyres there's no reason why a high-performance aluminium bike can't be tuned for all-day riding. Even the saddle can help damp out vibes from the back end of an aluminium frame. At one time it was also possible to acquire frames built with an aluminium main triangle with carbon fibre seat and chainstays engineered to absorb road vibes through the back wheel. A carbon fork did the same thing for the front end.

→ Compliant wheels and tyre combinations can make a big difference to the ride comfort of an aluminium frame.

← Titanium became popular with professional racers in the 1990s.

→ Titanium has been making a comeback recently with classy machines from big brands and custom builders.

## Titanium

First used in a bicycle frame in the 1950s, titanium made a brief appearance in the Tour de France in the early 1970s before some enterprising US frame builders finally overcame its tricky properties to establish titanium as a superlative material for bikes in the 1990s.

Titanium is pricey. It's difficult to work and weld and unless the correct grades are used for the butted tubes, it can be overly flexible in a frame. Merlin and Litespeed overcame all of the above apart from the cost, as a result of which only professionals and dedicated cyclists chose to ride titanium frames when they came of age in the 1990s.

Titanium racing frames for road and time trials were used by top professionals in that decade and the bikes produced were very light, comfortable and completely resistant to corrosion. In theory titanium has the longest life of all frame-building materials, but carbon frames are lighter and more affordable, and fans of titanium rapidly dwindled as the 21st century dawned. Racing cyclists never came back, but tourists and sportive riders have come to appreciate the comfort and performance offered by titanium frames, and as prices have come down numerous frame builders and manufacturers today offer bespoke and off-the-peg frames and machines.

## Carbon fibre

America's three-time Tour de France winner Greg LeMond used a French Look bike with a carbon frame to win his first Tour in 1986, the first time a composite frame was used to take victory in the world's most prestigious bike race. That signalled the start of the carbon-fibre revolution. But it was a slow start, as manufacturers experimented with various methods of fabricating frames from this wonder material, previously associated only with the aerospace industry and Grand Prix racing.

Success in the Tour de France represented the pinnacle of the sport, and the winning bike would often be the machine that hobby riders lusted after and could be found in bike shops just months later. Consequently by the 2000s carbon bikes had

virtually taken over the pro race paddock and customer versions were becoming increasingly available and, more importantly, affordable. Gone were round carbon tubes bonded into chunky looking lugs, replaced mostly by monocoque or semi-monocoque frames of complex shapes that made the most of carbon's ability

→ Since the late 1990s carbon fibre has dominated pro race bike manufacture.

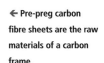

**Carbon fibre remains the material of choice for top-end road bikes.**

**Pre-preg carbon fibre sheets are the raw materials of a carbon frame.**

**Carbon can be engineered to flex or in couplings designed to offer several millimetres of deflection.**

**Carbon fibre frames can crack and fail, so be sure you're buying from a reputable brand.**

to be 'tuned' to suit the contrasting stresses and demands on key areas of the frame.

After more than a century of the diamond frame constructed with skinny tubes, mostly steel, these hi-tech and arresting machines began to attract many new admirers seduced into buying a bike instead of a new set of golf clubs.

Carbon-fibre frames and complete bikes dominate the high-end road market, with quality machines starting at £1,000 while upwards of £8,000 will get you a bike as good as or even lighter than a Tour de France machine. Carbon is light and strong, it doesn't fatigue like a metal frame and there are even craftsmen who can repair a damaged frame.

The raw carbon is usually supplied to the manufacturer in sheets pre-pregnated with resin, which is then cut and laid into moulds. How the carbon is laid up, its thickness and the direction of the fibres (either weave or the more popular unidirectional) all determine the ultimate performance of the frame.

As expertise has grown in the art of engineering and laying-up carbon frames the best brands are able to create frames which are incredibly stiff around the bottom bracket area and head tube while offering some welcome flex along the seat stays and forks. Carbon frames can even be manufactured with bump-absorbing couplings with dampers inserted that in effect are mini suspension units.

Carbon is almost the perfect material for bicycle frames and parts, but that does mean you should seek it out exclusively or over and above other equally effective materials. As with anything popular, there are inevitably second-rate imitations and even fakes out there that underperform the real thing to a serious and sometimes dangerous degree.

Low-quality carbon laid inexpertly into an out-dated mould can weigh as much as an aluminium frame and offer a hard and unforgiving ride. Carbon can also fail, especially across the joints of a semi-monocoque frame. Don't be deceived by its appearance, as it can be very hard to tell a quality frame from a cheap pretender, or even a direct rip-off of an established model from a respected brand. If it's for sale at a great price on an auction website, beware! Do you really want to go into a speed wobble on a 50mph descent for the sake of a bargain price?

# How bicycle frames are made

## Welding

Welding is the best way to join tubes of aluminium and titanium as well as steel, although the last lends itself equally well to filet brazing and joints with lugs. Welding with tungsten inert gas (TIG) creates an almost invisible join that makes it look like the mitred tubes are just touching. Only the smallest line of filler can be observed on steel and titanium frames, while on aluminium the filler rod (using the same material as the frame) can be used to make either a smooth or rippled joint.

 TIG welding is the most common way to join frames of aluminium and titanium.

## Brazing

Only used for steel frames with lugs or for lugless construction with steel tubes. Brazing joins the lug to the tube or the ends of mitred tubes by melting brass or silver filler at a lower temperature than the tubes or lugs. The filler is drawn into the lug by capillary reaction. On a lugless frame the excess filler can be finished to create the cleanest of joins, which is in contrast to the more ornate finishing on a plain or fancy lug.

## Bonding

Bonding may not be very common in the production of tubed aluminium and carbon frames any more, but carbon-fibre semi-monocoque frames use bonding agents or adhesives to join different elements together, and bonded inserts are common for bottle cages, guides, gear hangers and bottom brackets. Carbon fork blades can be bonded to an aluminium steerer via the carbon shoulder of the fork. Carbon stays can also be bonded to the bottom bracket junction or top end of the seat cluster.

↑ A very smooth joint can be created by brazing with brass or silver.

↓ Bonding is commonly used on carbon frames for threaded inserts.

# Wheels and tyres

← A pair of hand-built wheels can transform the performance of a bike.

dangerously expensive obsession with desirable and exclusive rims, spokes and hubs!

And if you do buy or already have a bike with wheels that are either sub-standard to the machine or worn out, or you just want to upgrade to something better, it's a relatively easy and enjoyable process to replace them.

## Rims

Wheel rims attract a great deal of attention, their modern aerodynamic profiles and carbon-fibre construction contributing greatly to the look of the machine as a whole. They're typically made from aluminium with an anodised finish, and on quality versions a hardened braking surface if used with caliper brakes.

Carbon rims are found on high-performance lightweight road wheels and are favoured for their low weight and suitability for deep-sided, V-section construction. They're strong too, and have proved themselves on wheels built for professional riders in cobbled-road classic one-day races, like Paris–Roubaix.

Deep-section carbon rims also offer an aero advantage over conventional wheels and most manufacturers offer varying depths of rim right up to a full disc wheel constructed entirely of carbon. At the other end of the scale are ultra-lightweight rims designed for climbing, with minimal carbon rims and spoking.

The number of holes in the rim can affect its weight and strength and typically range from 12 to 36. The rear wheel has a lot more to do than the front as it supports most of the weight of the rider, transmits pedalling power to the road and is constructed with an asymmetric 'dish' to accommodate the cassette and sprockets. The rim at the rear may have a higher number of spoke holes as it bears more weight and drivetrain forces than the front wheel.

## Wheels

After the frame the wheels are the most important part of a bike. Not only are they approximately one quarter of the total weight of the machine but the quality and specification of the wheels also have a marked effect on the ride and handling of the bike. Yet wheels are often overlooked when purchasing a bike. Comprised of a mass of spokes and usually a skinny rim, the wheels don't make the same impression as the frame, the gears and other interesting and colourful items like the saddle and handlebars.

After the frame it's said that cyclists looking for a new bike regard the rear derailleur as a key component in the decision-making process. Rear derailleurs in similar price bands operate as well as each other and these days almost without exception they work brilliantly well. But not so wheels, which can vary greatly within the same price range and will greatly affect the feel of the bike, much more than the derailleurs.

It pays, literally, to take an interest in wheels, as a good pair that suit your riding style, weight and tastes will enhance your bike and rides no end. Beware, though – it's easy to develop a

↓ Deep-section carbon wheels have proved themselves in the toughest road races.

↓ Modern wheels have wider rims to accommodate tyres from 25c upwards.

↑ A conventionally spoked wheel with spokes laced into a small flange hub.

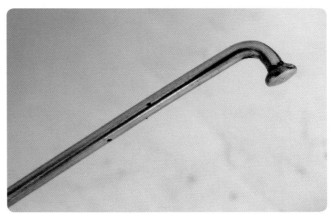

↑ Traditional steel spoke showing the J-bend which threads into the hub.

Rims intended for wheels built with disc brakes don't need a machined or treated braking track and can be shaped more freely. In theory a lighter rim can be used with a disc brake set-up, although in practice the advantages are outweighed by the additional weight of the hub, disc and carrier.

## Spokes

Steel or stainless steel wire spokes have been used to build bicycle wheels since the 1870s, when it was found that tensioned spokes pulling on a hub could hold a rim in compression capable of supporting many times the weight of bike and rider. That remains the case today and wheels manufactured or built by hand using steel spokes remain very much the norm on bikes of every type and quality.

A traditional steel spoke is a length of wire threaded at one end, with a J-bend at the other topped with a mushroom-shaped head. The curved end sits in a hole in the hub flange while the threaded end is located in double eyelets on an alloy rim, held in place by a threaded nipple that can be screwed in or out to adjust the tension of the spoke. As long as the spoke J-bend rests against the edge of the flange and the wheel is built with just the right amount of tension, the spoke head won't flex and should give many years of trouble-free service.

↓ Wheels with straight-pull spokes can be stiffer and lighter than a conventional wheel.

Straight-pull steel spokes do without the J-bend and must be laced on to an appropriately designed hub where the domed head sits directly opposite the rim rather than angled out to one side. It's still important that the wheel is built correctly, as any misalignment can lead to excessive spoke flex and eventually breakages.

Steel spokes can be butted at the hub end or at both ends (double-butted). The middle of the spoke is thinner and stretches further than a plain-gauge spoke when the wheel is tensioned. This is a good thing as it allows the spoke to contract a little more when the rim is compressed, in a pothole for instance.

Spokes can also be made from aluminium or carbon and can be flattened or elliptical in shape. Stronger, more rigid rims are used when less flexible materials are employed or when the spoke count drops below about 28 and the result can be a very rigid wheel that goes wildly out of true if a spoke fails.

## Hubs

At the centre of the wheel the hub anchors the spokes, has bearings on either side of the barrel and is fixed to the bike via its axle, using either nuts or a quick-release skewer. There are many different types of hub, with various spoking options, flange sizes and materials.

↓ A conventional hub showing the sealed bearings and spoke holes in the flanges.

↑ Traditional cup-and-cone bearings still have a lot going for them.

↓ The quick-release skewer passes through the hollow spindle of the hub.

↓ Hub for use with a disc brake, showing the threaded disc carrier.

Most bearings in quality modern hubs are annular or sealed cartridge types that are pressed into the hub and can easily be replaced when they wear out. Annular bearings are widely available and can be ordered either as bike parts or from a bearing supplier, using the part number on the side of the bearing. Quality can vary and there may also be options for heavy-duty seals or bearings made from steel or ceramic.

Traditional cup-and-cone bearings with loose ball bearings running in a race or cup and adjusted with the cone are still very much in use and can be found on hubs from Shimano and Campagnolo. This type of bearing may sound more complicated and fiddly but the ability to unscrew the cones and remove and re-grease the ball bearings can greatly extend its service life compared to annular bearings. Cup-and-cone bearings also resist loads from the side much more effectively than annular bearings.

Running through the centre of the hub is the spindle, which is usually made from steel but can also be aluminium, often oversize and housed in a fatter-barrelled hub body. The spindle is hollow if wheel closure is with a quick-release skewer. It passes through the spindle and is secured with a lever and threaded nut, clamped to the frame fork ends or rear dropouts.

On a track bike or fixed-wheel road bike the wheels are usually bolted in place, allowing for a solid spindle. Quick-release skewers are mostly made from steel with alloy or steel levers and bolts, but lightweight titanium or all-alloy versions can save a few precious grams. Some aftermarket wheels are supplied without the quick-release, and of course they don't come with tyres or cassette either.

Hubs intended for use with disc brakes must have a disc carrier machined on one side, and this extra material inevitably adds weight. The extra forces exerted through the disc brake have also led to the development of the through-axle, which features an oversize axle that either screws directly into one side of the fork or the rear end or is clamped in place with pinch bolts.

The hub body can be made from steel, alloy, titanium or carbon fibre, which are progressively lower in weight but higher in price. Much depends on the overall construction and materials used for the wheel but the most common hubs are made from alloy, which offers the best combination of strength and low weight. Alloy is also the best material for pressed-in annular bearings.

## Freehubs

On multi-geared road bikes the rear hub can accommodate up to 11 sprockets, and the freehub-style body invented by Shimano is by far the most popular in use today. Introduced in the 1970s, the freehub's advantages over a traditional freewheel composed of six or seven sprockets with an integral freewheel mechanism were appreciated immediately.

Not only did the freehub make removal and replacement of individual sprockets a lot easier, it also allowed the drive-side bearing to be moved further outboard, virtually eliminating the stresses on traditional axles used with freewheels. The design of the cassette freehub, a splined sprocket carrier with the freewheel

→ Shimano's freehub design has been universally adopted.

inside and attached to the hub, also eliminated the ingress of water and grit that caused damage and failures to freewheels.

Removal of the sprockets from a freehub is simply a matter of undoing a lock-ring on the end of the sprockets and then sliding sprockets and spacers off the splines of the cassette. Gone are the days of skinned knuckles and mashed dogs which threatened every removal of a freewheel and block.

Cassette sprockets must match the splines of the cassette, often determined by the brand, and the number of sprockets must also correspond to the specification of the hub, which typically will range from eight to eleven.

Sprockets are mostly made from steel, which is the best material by far for strength and longevity. Alloy sprockets are light but more prone to wear and titanium sprockets are expensive, and it makes more sense to save weight in the rims and tyres than in the centre of the wheel where centrifugal forces are negligible.

↓ Individual sprockets can be changed on a freehub cassette.

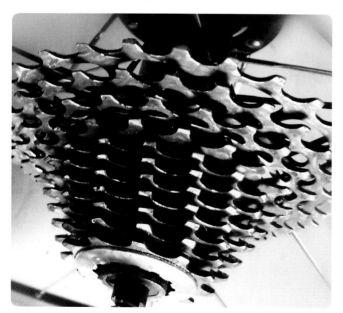

### Aero wheels

One of the most popular upgrades to a road bike are the wheels, which makes a lot of sense as a lighter, faster pair of wheels can transform a bike. Many bikes come with wheels that cause the frame and components to underperform. Manufacturers will often economise on the wheelset to ensure an attractive price point with above-average frame or parts. After a year or so of riding it's not uncommon for a pair of budget wheels to begin showing signs of wear or to go out of true due to a poor build.

A pair of aerodynamic wheels will greatly enhance the appearance of the bike as well as offer a significant gain in performance, as proven in wind-tunnel testing. Aero wheels rank high on the list of key elements – riding position being top – that reduce wind resistance. If you're a road cyclist who wants to average speeds in the high teens and beyond, aero wheels are the most important piece of bike-mounted kit to save up for.

↓ Many road bikes come with wheels that can be upgraded.

↑ A road bike with aero wheels will go faster and looks good too.

↓ Deep-section aero wheels can be used for road or time trial racing depending on the depth of the rim.

When we talk about aero wheels we're really referring to aero rims and possibly spokes. Aero V-shaped rims made from aluminium were developed in the 1980s, with Campagnolo's Shamal deep-section aero wheels the first off-the-peg high-performance road wheels in the 1990s. Carbon rims with similar profiles soon followed and the reduced weight over aluminium allowed even deeper profiles to be developed.

Today deep-section carbon rims up to 95mm deep are used for road riding and can even be very effective on time trial and triathlon bikes, especially in crosswinds when a full-disc wheel on the back is too unstable. For the ultimate non-disc aero road wheel there are three- to five-spoke full carbon wheels, which are expensive, very stiff but super aero.

Carbon aero wheels are generally available for tubular and clincher or wired-on tyres. The rim bed shape for tubular tyre compatibility is simpler, with just a shallow valley required for the tyre to sit in whereas the raised sides required for a clincher tyre are more complicated to manufacture. As a result there are many carbon aero rims that use an alloy rim with a carbon V-shaped fairing bonded to it. Carbon rims have benefited greatly from wind-tunnel testing and computer-aided design, with more rounded profiles, golf-ball type dimples and extra width all helping to smooth out the airflow from the tip of the rim to the leading edge of the tyre.

## Wheel sizes

By far the most popular wheel size for road bikes is '700c'. Most road and hybrid bikes have 700c wheels. On mountain bikes the 29in wheel has become fashionable in recent times and it's possible to swap wheel types between machines fitted with disc brakes and 29in or 700c wheels.

700c is today the standard size for wheels fitted with clincher or tubular tyres. Older, pre-1980 road bikes were commonly fitted with 27in wheels, which are slightly bigger than 700c (bead seat diameter 630mm for 27in and 622mm for 700c). Some road trekking bikes, bespoke tourers, tandems and mountain bikes run on the smaller 650b wheel size (584mm bead seat diameter). Wheelsets can be light and very comfortable when riding on fat road tyres run at below-average pressures.

## Tyres

Often overlooked and outshone by more exciting components, the tyres on a bike play a number of vital roles, from determining ride comfort to providing confidence-inspiring grip in the wet. A bicycle sits on two contact patches smaller than a postage stamp. On a road bike expected to offer a supple ride, corner downhill at speeds well over 30mph, lean over in the wet and grip consistently under braking, trusting all that to budget rubber is, to say the least, foolhardy.

Modern lightweight quality road tyres for general riding and racing offer excellent grip, puncture protection and ride quality. If there's one consumable on your bike for which the price should be a secondary consideration, it's a good pair of tyres.

Economy tyres are, ironically, a false economy. With less threads per inch (TPI) in their construction they'll ride stiffly and transmit less feedback to the rider. They probably won't have a puncture protection band and will therefore be more susceptible to punctures. Cheaper rubber will wear out more quickly and offer less grip in the wet.

There are many quality brands of tyre and it's worth taking a little time to do some research before upgrading to a new set. First consider the bike on which the tyres will be used. If it's an all-year machine used for winter riding and summer challenge rides there are some excellent four-seasons tyres which offer above-average levels of handling and performance, as well as hard-wearing rubber tread compounds and puncture resistance.

For a summer road bike, when most rides will be on dry roads free from grit, the choices are more racy and can include lighter tyres right up to racing-standard rubber. Puncture protection will be less but the gains in handling and feel are worth it. Reducing the weight in the tyre and inner tube also lowers the rotating weight at the rim, making acceleration much zippier.

For a winter bike there are training tyres that can go for months without puncturing or wearing excessively. A Kevlar puncture protection band helps but there's no need to go for heavily treaded tyres as it's a myth that they offer more grip or water dispersal than a lightly treaded or even slick tyre.

A heavily treaded or knobbly tyre will grip in mud but not so well on metalled roads. If anything traction is reduced, because there's less rubber in contact with the road. There can even be quite unnerving movements caused by the deflection of raised blocks on a cyclo-cross or MTB-style road tyre.

Water dispersal on a bicycle tyre doesn't require the elaborately patterned sipes seen on motorcycle and car tyres, where the width of the tyre traps water between the rubber and the road. Without sipes literally siphoning the water to the outside a car tyre will aquaplane, causing a catastrophic loss of control.

The contact patch on a bicycle tyre is small enough to push water around the sides. There's no need to channel water from under the contact patch and then out through the sides. Grip is determined by the quality of the compounds used in the tread, and that's why a slick bicycle tyre can grip better than a treaded version in the wet.

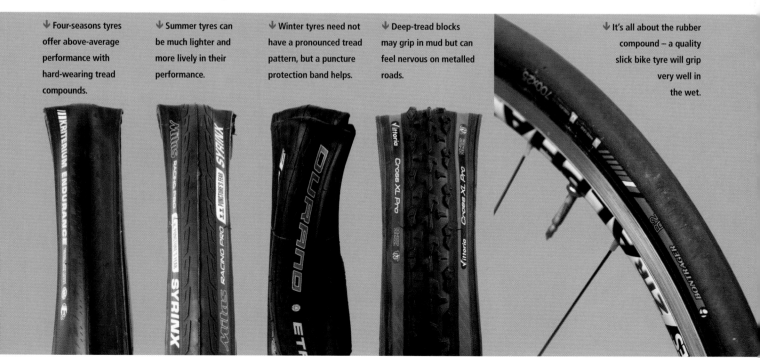

⬇ Four-seasons tyres offer above-average performance with hard-wearing tread compounds.

⬇ Summer tyres can be much lighter and more lively in their performance.

⬇ Winter tyres need not have a pronounced tread pattern, but a puncture protection band helps.

⬇ Deep-tread blocks may grip in mud but can feel nervous on metalled roads.

⬇ It's all about the rubber compound – a quality slick bike tyre will grip very well in the wet.

# Tyre sizes, widths and pressures

The tyre size should correspond to the size of the wheel, which for a road bike will normally be 700/622 (700c/622mm). On the side of the tyre or on the packaging the tyre size will be displayed

→ Tyre information is displayed on the sidewall.

← A tyre of 25c or more can ride at lower pressures with no loss of rolling resistance.

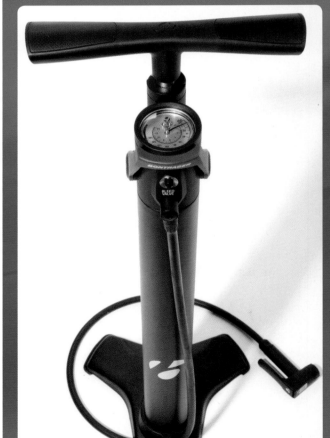

as '700c x 23c' or '23-622', the 23 referring to the tyre width. Tyre width will give an indication as to the volumetric size of the tyre, which for road bikes can range from 18c to 35c.

Wider rim widths on quality wheels have made tyres of 25c or even bigger very popular in recent times. Running a fatter tyre at lower pressures can greatly enhance the comfort of the ride with little effect on the rolling resistance. It's a fallacy that a narrower tyre rolls faster than a fatter version. If the pressures and construction are the same the fatter tyre suffers from less deflection, resulting in lower rolling resistance than a skinny tyre.

Tyre pressure depends on the type of tyre, the weight of the rider and the state of the roads. It's well worth experimenting with different tyre pressures, typically on a road tyre from 70–120psi (4.8–8.2bar). The pressure limits of the tyre should be marked on the sidewall, and the only way to achieve higher pressures is with a track or floor-mounted stirrup pump with a gauge in psi or bar.

Pumping the tyre up to its maximum can result in a harsh ride and won't make the bike any faster.

← Use a stirrup pump with a gauge to ensure tyres are pumped to the desired pressure.

↑ **High-quality performance clinchers feel light and supple in the hand.**

## Clincher or wired-on tyres

The most common type of bike tyre, the clincher is an open cover with a steel or synthetic bead that, when mounted and inflated around an inner tube on the rim, engages with a hook running around the rim sides. The carcass of the tyre is made up of thin layers of fabric, either natural or man-made, laid in plies with the individual threads running perpendicular to each other.

The quality and quantity of the threads is indicated by the number of threads per inch, marked as 'TPI' on the sidewall or technical data sheet. The greater the number, the more supple and responsive the tyre.

Exotic materials can be used to reduce the weight and improve the performance of a clincher tyre. Kevlar beads and puncture protection strips, aramid carcasses and twin-compound

← **Use inner tubes with presta valves and make sure the valve stem is long enough for your rims.**

treads can all add to the desirability of a clincher tyre. Just picking up and handling a tyre can tell you a lot about the weight and suppleness of the materials used.

Inner tubes should match the tyre for size and width, and don't forget to use the presta valve version which is standard fitment on road rims with smaller holes. Presta valves have to be opened before air is added and that involves carefully unscrewing a little barrel down a threaded metal stalk poking out of the valve body. Care must be taken not to bend this stalk or when pushing on the head of the pump. It's worth paying extra for a quality lightweight inner tube to go with light clincher tyres, as the tube will keep the total rotating weight down and move better with the tyre.

## Tubeless tyres

Clincher tyres without an inner tube, tubeless tyres are popular on mountain bikes but remain a niche interest on the road. Tubeless tyres can only be used with a dedicated tubeless rim, which resembles a regular clincher rim with raised sides and a hook to retain the tyre. But instead of rim tape covering the spoke heads the tubeless rim has an additional aluminium or carbon bed above the spokes, creating a sealed chamber when the tyre is fitted and inflated. Pressure in the tyre, combined with the airtight rim, ensures that no air can escape. Small punctures can be plugged instantly with tyre sealant.

There's much to be said for the tubeless tyre, but the conservative world of cycling has been slow to abandon the almost universal clincher and

→ **A tubeless rim is airtight once the tyre is inflated.**

↑ Tubeless tyres have much to recommend them but they've been slow to catch on.

tube tyre and rim combination. It's true that tubeless tyres can be difficult to mount on the rim but once in place they perform at least as well as the best clincher tyres.

Some manufacturers call their tubeless tyres 'open tubular' and in some ways the tubeless tyre combines the low weight and suppleness of a tubular tyre with the ease of fitment and repair of a clincher. If rim and tyre manufacturers continue to develop their tubeless options the future could be a lot brighter for the open tubular.

## Tubular tyres

Well over a century old, the tubular tyre refuses to die despite being the only component of a bike that requires several layers of sticky glue prior to use. In professional cycling the tubular tyre – also known as a 'tub' or 'sew-up' – remains the tyre of choice, combining excellent feel and comfort with low weight, a strong

↓ A tubular tyre is mounted on a simple 'sprint' rim using several layers of tubular-specific glue.

rim and the unusual plus of staying on the rim after a puncture.

The last is a particular concern for pros, who need to carry on riding on a flat tyre to minimise time lost on the bunch. By contrast a punctured clincher loses its shape and deforms rapidly, bringing the raised sides of the rim dangerously close to the road. Most of the time the rider brings the bike to a halt in short order without crashing. When a tubular tyre goes flat the tyre rests between the road and the rim, preventing the rim from making contact with the road.

The term 'sew-up' describes the tubular tyre well: it's basically a clincher tyre with the bead removed, sewn together into a sausage-like tube. The inner tube is encased in the carcass of the tyre, which is constructed the same way as a lightweight clincher type. A base tape is glued to the underside of the tyre, covering the stitched-up carcass, and this tape takes a layer or two of specialist rim cement before being carefully mounted on a 'sprint' rim with a shallow U-shaped bed, also coated in at least two layers of cement. Sticky tub tape can also be used to mount a tubular tyre.

The rim for a tubular is simpler and stronger than a clincher rim; it's also less susceptible to pinch flats, allowing tubs to be run at lower pressures than clincher tyres. Pressures in the low 20s psi can be used for cyclo-cross tubs, which makes them the default choice for serious off-road competition. At the other end of the scale tubs can also be pumped up to 200psi, which gives them a major performance advantage over clinchers for track racing.

For normal riding, challenge events and amateur road racing and time trialling the hassle and expense of tubulars outweighs the marginal performance advantages they offer over clinchers. For most riders the decider will be that tubular tyres don't roll faster than an equivalent high-quality clincher tyre pumped to the same pressure.

It used to be the case that top-end carbon rims could only be used with tubular tyres, mainly due to the more complicated rim shape for clinchers. But there are now many brands of lightweight carbon wheels of every type with clincher-friendly rims.

→ Strong and light, a sprint rim doesn't have the raised sides of the clincher rim.

# Gears

↑ On a 'penny-farthing' the bigger the wheel the further it rolls per single revolution.

↑ Riding a fixed-wheel or single-speed bike is a surprisingly fun and satisfying experience.

From one gear to dozens, the history of the bike has seen a gradual evolution in the number of gears available to the cyclist. The 'penny-farthing' is the most visual demonstration of what one gear ratio represents, as one turn of the pedals propels the big wheel exactly the circumference of that wheel, whatever its size. The bigger the wheel, the further the bike will travel per revolution of the pedals. But the rider has to pedal harder as the wheel gets bigger. For every pedal stroke the wheel exacts its price!

The principle is the same on a multi-geared modern bike, with a cluster of different-sized sprockets on the back wheel and a chainset with one, two or three rings of different sizes on the front. Each combination of chainset ring and sprocket will give a different ratio, expressed in the inches travelled for each pedal revolution. Imagine the smaller sprockets turning an ever-increasing wheel size – it's no different to the 'penny-farthing' wheel.

Do you need gears? Yes, but one can suffice if you favour a single fixed gear, which can be incredibly satisfying and efficient to pedal, especially on flat roads. Most riders opt for multiple gears, of course, but more is not always better and there's a place in everyone's collection for a fixed-wheel bike, which is the purest and most traditional pedalling experience in cycling.

## Double, triple and single speed chainsets

'Chainset' is the collective term for the assembly of bottom bracket, cranks and chainrings. It's where the power from both legs is transmitted to the back wheel, via a sprocket or cluster of gears.

A double or triple chainset refers to the number of chainrings attached to the crank with Allen bolts, usually via a four- or five-arm spider. Most cranks and chainrings are made from aluminium alloy, for its low weight and comparative stiffness and because chainrings made of this material have been found to wear better than steel.

↓ Quality chainrings are machined from aluminium alloy and last a long time if cared for.

61

↑ Carbon can be used for cranks and spider arms but isn't suited to chainring teeth.

→ Double chainsets, with two chainrings, are the most popular choice on modern road bikes.

Being softer, aluminium 'mates' with the chain for an exact fit. It's also thought that dirt and oil grinding into the teeth actually causes the material to harden over time. A thicker aluminium chainring remains light and is stiffer than a thin steel one, which traditionally was braced to prevent it from flexing.

Carbon cranks are commonplace on top-end chainsets but carbon doesn't lend itself well to chainrings with delicate teeth. Alloy threaded inserts and splines are usually bonded to carbon cranks where pedals and bottom bracket axles are attached.

Steel crank arms and chainrings are associated with budget road bikes manufactured up to the 1980s and were the original material of choice on most road bikes, including competition machines, until the 1950s. The cranks were secured to the bottom bracket axle with a cotter-pin wedged down one side of the crank and sitting on flats created in both the pin and the axle. As long as the cotter-pin is fitted correctly, with a snug fit between crank and axle and the bolt done up tight, all is well. If it isn't, however, the crank can come loose and the resulting wear can irreparably damage the assembly.

Double chainsets are by far the most popular choice for road riding. The addition of an inner chainring bolted behind the big ring on the same spider adds negligible additional weight and doubles the choice of gears on offer.

Triple chainsets require an extra set of threaded bosses on the inside of the spider and are still popular with trekking cyclists who need an extra set of very low gears. But since the advent of 10- and 11-speed cassettes, as well as the compact and mid-compact drivetrains, 'triples' have fallen out of favour with leisure and sports road riders, who have all the gears they need on a wide-ratio cassette.

An interesting recent development has been the introduction by SRAM and Shimano of a dedicated single-ring chainset that works with an 11-speed cassette. When used with SRAM's X1 rear derailleur, every sprocket can be accessed and the range of sprockets is astounding, with a 10–42 tooth option.

↑ Triple chainsets can still be found on trekking, touring and hybrid road bikes.

↓ Older, budget bikes were fitted with cranks secured to the bottom bracket with cotter-pins.

↓ Single-ring chainsets with wide-ratio cassettes do away with the front derailleur.

### Fixed

A bike with a fixed gear has a chainset with a single chainring driving, via a chain, one sprocket screwed directly to the rear wheel. There's no freewheel on the sprocket – the rider must continue pedalling until the rear wheel is stationary.

Fixed-wheel is the purest and most original form of bicycle propulsion. It remains the only drivetrain system on track bikes and is popular with city cyclists and serious riders interested in honing their pedalling technique or just taking pleasure in the feel of riding 'fixed'.

It's possible to ride a single sprocket with an internal freewheel mechanism and many city riders do favour the flexibility this offers, but single-free isn't permitted on track bikes and it

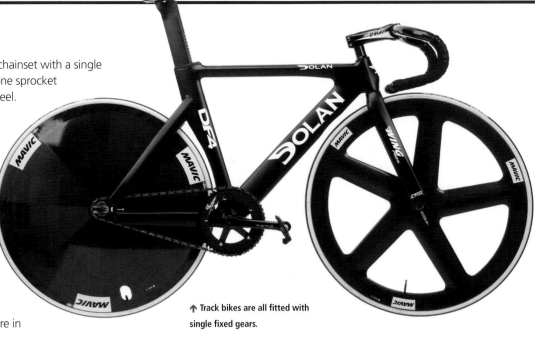

↑ Track bikes are all fitted with single fixed gears.

↓ A fixed-wheel training bike with mudguards makes a reliable and simple winter bike.

negates the feeling of momentum you get when riding a true fixed gear.

There's a certain mystique attached to road-going fixed-wheel bikes, as they appear to eschew the modern trend of offering dozens of gear ratios, available at the touch of a button or by minimal input from a complex and expensive drivetrain. For devotees the joy of riding fixed-wheel is derived precisely from its simplicity and the fact that, on flat or rolling terrain, one gear is enough if you're prepared to go up and down through a broader range of pedal revolutions. It's by no means impossible to match riders on geared bikes – even on hillier roads if you're strong on the uphills and manic on the descents!

It's possible to convert a standard road frame to fixed-wheel, but ideally the frame will have track ends or dropouts, which have a long slot open at the back along which the rear wheel can be adjusted back and forth to achieve the correct chain tension.

Using heavier duty ⅛inch track chainrings, sprockets and chains also extends the life of the drivetrain, although it's possible to use ³⁄₃₂inch standard road drivetrain components, which are lighter but less robust. Fixed-wheel training bikes with mudguards were very popular with club cyclists for many years thanks to their ease of maintenance, simplicity, low cost and benefits for pedalling technique and 'souplesse' (a French term meaning suppleness or flexibility; a rider who pedals with souplesse is admired for the fluid way his or her legs spin around, like a well-oiled machine).

### Compact, mid-compact and standard gears

For the last 20 years or so the industry standard for road bikes has been known as 'compact', which is basically a chainset with a 34-tooth inside ring and 50-tooth outside ring. When combined with a 10- or 11-speed cassette the compact drivetrain can access most of the gears required for all types of hills and everything but the fastest downhills.

⬆ Compact gearing is the most popular choice for general road riding and sportives.

⬆ Shimano were the first groupset brand to introduce electronic gear changing to the mass market.

Before the compact, riders who wanted a similar choice of gears had to fit a triple chainset, but the arrival of the compact drivetrain kicked triples into touch virtually overnight. Mid-compact gears offer a halfway house between compact and the traditional standard gearing of 53x39 (or before that 52x42). The mid-compact chainset has rings of 52 and 36 teeth.

## Which gear system for me?

Choosing the correct chainset and cassette combination isn't as difficult as it looks, because there are many shared ratios available between all three systems. With 10- and 11-speed cassettes offering sprockets from 11 to 32 teeth, and sprockets stacked in favour of larger or smaller gears depending on your preference, it's often a case of simply ensuring that the smallest gear suits the biggest hills you're likely to encounter. Top gear is less important – on a compact the 50x11 or 50x12 sprocket will have you panting on the flat.

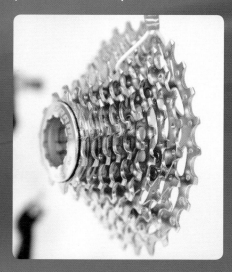

➔ Modern 10- and 11-speed cassettes offer a wide range of gear choices.

### Manual or electronic shifting?

Electronic gears ('E-gears') were once little more than a curiosity but have rapidly become the norm on many high-end road bikes. Most professionals race on bikes equipped with E-gears, and as the technology has become increasingly accepted and its few teething problems solved, even mid-priced road bikes can be specified with electronic gears. All three major component brands – Shimano (Di2), Campagnolo (EPS) and SRAM (eTap) – have E-groupsets in their ranges, with SRAM pushing the technology even further with their wireless system that makes fitting and maintenance easier still.

Shimano was the first to produce E-gears, introducing their Dura-Ace 7970 Di2 system to pro racing and soon after to the mass market in 2009. Campagnolo debuted its EPS system in 2012 and SRAM came late to the party in 2015. By then the first two had trickled down E-gear componentry to their mid-range groupsets, with the prospect of even more affordable versions around the corner.

➔ Electronic gear changes work particularly well on the front changer.

↑ A control unit indicates how much power is left in the battery.

↑ Cable-operated gears still have much to recommend them and almost match E-gears for ease of use.

Right from the start electronic gear changes offered fast and slick cog swaps, with automatic micro adjustment ensuring the rear derailleur never went out of sync. A well set-up cable derailleur comes close to E-gears when going 'down' the cassette, but where E-gears score is how they perform under load going both 'down' and especially 'up' the cassette. Most impressive is the performance of the front derailleur, which under E-power seems to defy physics when moving the chain from the small to the big chainring. A certain amount of finesse is still required when changing up on the front derailleur with a cable system.

E-gear batteries can go for many months between charges and every system has a power display that gives plenty of warning when a recharge is required. There's negligible weight difference between equivalent E-groupsets, and professional-level bikes equipped with E-gears easily get down to the UCI (Union Cycliste Internationale, or International Cycling Union) weight limit of 6.8kg.

Setting up electronic gears is relatively simple: once the cables have been routed through the frame it's simply a case of plugging them into the front and rear derailleurs. Unlike the traditional Bowden cable, which wears over time and requires adjustment or replacement, the electronic version should last many years.

Though E-gears are very good indeed, so are conventional derailleurs operated with cables, and for a great many cyclists the enhanced looks and ethos of electronic gears fail to outweigh the lower price, greater simplicity, 'feel' and tradition of manually operated gear changes. For them the traditional cable-operated derailleur will never be bettered, and who would argue against nearly a century of evolution? It's safe to say that, while E-gears are here to stay and offer marginally better performance, conventional cable-operated gears are far from obsolete.

→ Thin cables on E-gears plug directly into the front and rear derailleurs.

# Cranks

The crank is the lever attached to both sides of the bottom bracket. On the drive side it normally has stubby arms or a spider on to which the chainrings are bolted. On the non-drive side the crank is a simple-looking arm with holes both ends for the bottom bracket axle and pedal.

It's true that the pedals are the most direct interface between rider and machine, but the cranks are more important in terms of how a rider experiences the transfer of power from legs to bike. Crank length, as marked on the inside of both cranks either in the material itself or with a sticker, is one of the key factors in setting up a bike to suit the rider. Even small differences in crank length can have a marked effect on cadence and feel.

Normally crank length is determined by the rider's leg length. Cranks are measured in millimetres and typically range from 165mm through to 170, 172.5, 175 and 180mm. For banked tracks the 165mm crank is universal for most events, but on the road it also suits women or men with shorter legs. A shorter crank makes a smaller circle and can be revved faster, which is why the 165mm standard is best suited to fast pedalling, especially on single fixed gears.

The most common crank lengths found on road bikes are 170, 172.5 and 175mm. Most regular-sized road bikes for men will come with 172.5mm cranks, but the larger sizes may be fitted with 175s. These days 170mm cranks tend to be found on older machines.

It pays to make a note of your bike's crank length and to think about how it feels. Like saddle height, it's perfectly possible to ride comfortably at heights and lengths either side of your base settings. If you ride a mountain bike, for instance, the set-up can be quite radically different. After dropping the saddle height to compensate for the extra few millimetres, a pair of longer cranks will describe a bigger circle, bringing your knees closer to your

↑ Crank length in millimetres is indicated on the inside of the crank arm.

chest and extending the leg further forward and behind at the three and nine o'clock pedalling positions. At the bottom of the stroke there'll be no difference as long as the saddle has been adjusted.

It's possible to achieve a high pedalling cadence on longer cranks but it can take time and practice to get used to how it feels to rotate the legs through a bigger circle. Of course, the converse is also true; if you prefer a slower cadence then longer cranks can feel more comfortable to push.

For riders with very long or short legs crank length will be a key factor in their ability to pedal effectively. For average-sized riders the range of crank lengths above could all be perfectly rideable. Crank length can be a personal thing, based on feel, or it may be determined by a specific performance imperative, like riding a track or time-trial bike. That's why it's always well worth checking the length of the cranks on the bike you're riding.

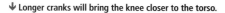
↓ Longer cranks will bring the knee closer to the torso.

↓ Shorter riders may favour cranks of 170mm or less.

# Nine, ten and eleven-speed cassettes

➔ Five-speed cogsets were common in the 1970s.

Until the 1970s the most common gear cluster or cogset comprised five sprockets. What prevented additional sprockets being added was the inboard location of the bearings on a traditional hub and freewheel, which resulted in stresses being transferred to the axle, especially when the chain was running on the smaller sprockets. Most keen cyclists of that period were familiar with the loss of drive after a rear axle had failed.

When the cassette hub was introduced its design enabled the rear wheel bearings to be placed further apart than the old freewheel. A much wider load-bearing axle could handle extra sprockets without stressing the axle, and the potential for extra sprockets resulted in something of a sprockets arms race between the two main component manufacturers at the time, Campagnolo and Shimano. From the 1980s on sprockets were increased, from six to nine by the 1990s, with 10- and 11-speed cassettes in the 2000s. Every extra sprocket was added by narrowing the gaps between them and producing ever slimmer (and more expensive) chains.

Traditional freewheels that may number seven or eight sprockets still feature on some budget road bikes. At the next price point a machine may have a cassette rear hub with nine sprockets. A road bike suitable for training, challenge rides and racing should be equipped with a ten-speed cassette, and these are standard on all entry-level quality groupsets from Shimano, Campagnolo and SRAM.

## Gearing steps

It's natural to place more importance on the size of the chainrings than the individual sprocket sizes in the cassette. Mostly it's the biggest and smallest sprockets that determine how the ones in between are spaced in order to achieve a relatively linear progression through the gears. A very big sprocket may be a lifesaver on a ridiculously steep hill but it's well worth checking that the cassette isn't stacked in favour of the smallest gears.

The best possible progression through the gears is by one tooth at a time, which traditionally was known as a 'straight-through' block. On a 10- or 11-speed cassette, however, it's possible to create straight-through gears with a two-tooth increase only between the biggest couple of sprockets. Unless the cassette is for racing, a 12-tooth smallest sprocket is plenty even with a compact chainset.

➔ On mid-range and up modern road bikes 10- and 11-speed cassettes are the norm.

# Choosing upper and lower gears

| Cassette | Standard | | Compact | | Triple | | |
|---|---|---|---|---|---|---|---|
| | 53 | 39 | 50 | 34 | 50 | 39 | 30 |
| 11 | 4.82 | 3.55 | 4.55 | 3.09 | 4.55 | 3.55 | 2.73 |
| 12 | 4.42 | 3.25 | 4.17 | 2.83 | 4.17 | 3.25 | 2.50 |
| 13 | 4.08 | 3.00 | 3.85 | 2.62 | 3.85 | 3.00 | 2.31 |
| 14 | 3.79 | 2.79 | 3.57 | 2.43 | 3.57 | 2.79 | 2.14 |
| 15 | 3.53 | 2.60 | 3.33 | 2.27 | 3.33 | 2.60 | 2.00 |
| 16 | 3.31 | 2.44 | 3.13 | 2.13 | 3.13 | 2.44 | 1.88 |
| 17 | 3.12 | 2.29 | 2.94 | 2.00 | 2.94 | 2.29 | 1.76 |
| 18 | 2.94 | 2.17 | 2.78 | 1.89 | 2.78 | 2.17 | 1.67 |
| 19 | 2.79 | 2.05 | 2.63 | 1.79 | 2.63 | 2.05 | 1.58 |
| 20 | 2.65 | 1.95 | 2.50 | 1.70 | 2.50 | 1.95 | 1.50 |
| 21 | 2.52 | 1.86 | 2.38 | 1.62 | 2.38 | 1.86 | 1.43 |
| 22 | 2.41 | 1.77 | 2.27 | 1.55 | 2.27 | 1.77 | 1.36 |
| 23 | 2.30 | 1.70 | 2.17 | 1.48 | 2.17 | 1.70 | 1.30 |
| 24 | 2.21 | 1.63 | 2.08 | 1.42 | 2.08 | 1.63 | 1.25 |
| **25** | **2.12** | **1.56** | **2.00** | **1.36** | **2.00** | **1.56** | **1.20** |
| 26 | 2.04 | 1.50 | 1.92 | 1.31 | 1.92 | 1.50 | 1.15 |
| **27** | **1.96** | **1.44** | **1.85** | **1.26** | **1.85** | **1.44** | **1.11** |
| 28 | 1.89 | 1.39 | 1.79 | 1.21 | 1.79 | 1.39 | 1.07 |
| 29 | 1.83 | 1.34 | 1.72 | 1.17 | 1.72 | 1.34 | 1.03 |
| 30 | 1.77 | 1.30 | 1.67 | 1.13 | 1.67 | 1.30 | 1.00 |
| 31 | 1.71 | 1.26 | 1.61 | 1.10 | 1.61 | 1.26 | 0.97 |
| 32 | 1.66 | 1.22 | 1.56 | 1.06 | 1.56 | 1.22 | 0.94 |

↑ Gear ratio table.

## Campagnolo groupsets

- **Super Record** mechanical and electronic (EPS) – pro racing.
- **Record** mechanical and EPS – pro racing and sportives.
- **Chorus** mechanical and EPS – club racing and sportives.
- **Athena** – training and sportives.
- **Veloce** – entry-level sportives and winter training.

## Shimano groupsets

- **Dura-Ace** mechanical and electronic (Di2) – pro racing.
- **Ultegra** mechanical and Di2 – club racing and sportives.
- **105** – training and sportives.
- **Tiagra** – entry-level sportives and winter training.
- **Sora** – winter training and starter bikes.
- **Claris** – starter bikes.

↑ Campagnolo Super Record.

↑ Shimano Ultegra.

## SRAM groupsets

- **Red** mechanical and electronic (eTap) – pro racing.
- **Force** and single ring (CX1) – racing and sportives.
- **Rival** – training and sportives.
- **Apex** – hilly sportives and touring.

← SRAM Force.

# Brakes

↑ Rod brakes pulling up on the rim are still in use on utility bikes today.

↑ Cantilever brakes allow much fatter tyres to be fitted, although disc brakes do the same and perform with more feel and power.

Just about every type of braking system has been tried on a bike, from a crude spoon-shaped plunger pressing on the top of the tyre through to drum and disc brakes. In between came the rod or roller lever brake, which operated on the underside of the rim by pulling upwards via a steel rod and can still be found on some traditional utility bikes. But when the Endrick rim became commonplace its vertically sided braking surface was perfectly shaped for a brake system acting in compression and exacting enough force to lock the wheel. From the 1930s cable-operated rim brakes, in centre-pull or side-pull form, quickly became *de rigueur* on performance road bikes.

Both types of brake were relatively simple and light, and, crucially on a racing bike, allowed wheels to be removed without fouling the rim or tyre. The centre-pull design remained popular until the 1950s among racing cyclists and even longer on budget sports bikes.

Cantilever brakes, attached to bosses on the forks and tubes either side of the rim, offered extra clearance for cyclo-cross and touring bikes and are still in use today, especially on cyclo-cross racing bikes.

## Side-pull brake

The cable operated side-pull brake, attached with a bolt through the front fork crown and the same way through the rear brake bridge, is favoured by amateurs and professionals alike and has barely changed, at least outwardly, for the last 40 years. However, although visually sharing the same architecture as Campagnolo's benchmark Record caliper brake introduced in 1969, some significant improvements over the years have resulted in levels of power, progression and feel which remain hard to beat.

→ Side-pull caliper brakes have been around for decades and have only recently begun to lose ground to hydraulic disc brakes.

→ Campagnolo's Record side-pull brake marries form and function to perfection.

69

→ Shimano Dura-Ace caliper designed for use behind the bottom bracket.

↑ Direct-mount calipers are mounted to the stays and fork blades with two bolts.

↑ Aero road bikes feature centre-pull brakes that can be tucked away out of the airflow.

↓ Disc brakes are the norm on mountain bikes with suspension forks and fat tyres.

Dual-pivot calipers introduced by Shimano in the 1990s exerted welcome additional leverage on the rim, and were followed by advances in lever design that also increased the mechanical power of side-pull designs.

More recently direct-mount side-pull calipers, attached to the bike in a similar way to cantilevers, have reduced flex almost totally from the caliper lever arms. Add to all those advances the relative simplicity and low total weight of the cable-operated side-pull from brake lever to pads and it's not so surprising that they're still in use by a great many road cyclists, right up to professional level.

## Centre-pull brake

The centre-pull brake has made something of a comeback on aero road bikes and time trial bikes, where the rear brake is situated behind the bottom bracket, underneath the chainstays, and on the front fork where it's tucked inside the fork crown in front or behind the crown and sometimes behind an aerodynamic plate. Using a direct mount system with two mounting points on both sides of the caliper, the centre-pull brake can be rigidly attached and performs almost as well as a quality side-pull brake.

## Disc brake

Hydraulic disc brakes have revolutionised bike retardation. For the first time in decades, the cable-operated caliper brake has a serious adversary. Mountain bikers took to disc brakes immediately and few MTBs come without them fitted. Fatter knobbly tyres on mountain bikes and suspension front forks allow much harder braking, especially on softer terrain where a slide can be controlled, and the extra weight of the system is less of an issue on relatively heavy off-road machinery. As downhill mountain-biking has gained in popularity over cross-country, high performance disc brakes are seen as essential when careering down long technical descents.

On a road bike there are pros and cons to disc brakes that continue to divide opinion. Foremost is the additional weight, at least 800gm and considerably more if a budget cable-operated system is used. The frame and fork must also be fitted with mounting points, which can add weight, and a stronger fork may be required to soak up higher braking forces exerted on one side from the bottom of the fork blade.

Wheel rims can be lighter, as they don't need to provide a braking track for rim brakes, but the hubs must be designed with extra mounting points for the discs and the axles beefed up, or of the 'straight-through' variety, to prevent the stresses of higher braking forces. Then there's the argument that disc brakes offer too much braking power, which can all too easily overwhelm conventional road bike tyres. However, this is countered by higher levels of 'feel', which make disc brakes easier to modulate in all conditions.

In the wet, especially, disc brakes outperform rim brakes quite comprehensively as they aren't affected by water on the braking surface. In the heat discs perform just as well, but opponents claim that heat build-up in the disc material can cause nasty injuries in the event of a crash.

At professional level, where fast wheel changes can win or lose races, there's been concern about the more fiddly process of slotting the disc in between the brake pads, especially if the pads have been inadvertently compressed or knocked out of line. Through axles can also take longer to undo compared to the traditional skewer and quick-release lever.

↑ The frame and fork must be disc-brake compatible, with additional bosses for the calipers.

→ Hubs are machined with mounting points for the discs.

↓ Through axles (bottom) are threaded at one end and can take longer to secure than a traditional quick-release.

# Handlebars

↑ **Drop handlebars offer multiple hand positions, many more than flat bars used on hybrids and mountain bikes.**

One of the signature elements of a road bike is drop handlebars. Straight along the top, drop bars curve forward before making a half turn down and back. The 'hooks' of the drop handlebar come with many subtle variations but are essentially the same thing. Drop handlebars offer more hand positions than any other bar, giving the rider a choice of riding positions ranging from upright to crouched in an aerodynamic tuck.

Many beginners start out on mountain bikes and hybrids fitted with flat bars and it's easy to see the appeal of the extra width of the bars, comfy hand grips and brake levers that are easily to hand. Flat bars are undoubtedly enjoyable to use for short trips or rides on twisty tracks where the extra leverage on the bars and ease of pulling on the brakes scores over drop

↓ **Flat bars are comfortable for short rides but offer a limited range of riding positions.**

bars. On longer rides, however, the upright, fixed riding position imposed on the rider by flat bars becomes irksome, especially if riding into the wind. And while it may look more comfortable to sit in an upright riding position the resultant rearwards shift in weight distribution can increase discomfort on the seat.

In almost every respect drop handlebars are superior to flat, as they offer at least half-a-dozen hand positions, from the most upright in the centre of the bars to the lowest most aero position on the bottom of the 'drops'.

Working the vertical brake levers from the drops offers as much feel and control as on a flat-bar bike, with the added advantage of lowering the rider's centre of gravity for extra stability on corners and descents. Riding on the rubberised hoods of the brakes also allows the fingers to work the brake levers from above as well as providing all-day riding comfort in a semi-aero tuck.

Drop handlebars are also tuneable in terms of stack height, brake lever position and orientation in the stem clamp. Bars often come in a range of sizes to suit either the width of the rider's shoulders or personal preference for either narrow or wider-than-average widths. Finally, you get to choose the bar-tape colour, thickness and material, all of which can add to the riding comfort and aesthetics of your road bike.

↓ **Even on the brake hoods the rider can adopt a very aerodynamic tuck position.**

## Drop handlebar styles

### ➔ Classic

Italian manufacturer Cinelli introduced the first widely used aluminium drop handlebars in the 1960s and from then on alloy bars took over from steel as the bars of choice for serious road cyclists. Road bikes before that time had used various shapes of dropped bars, some with very shallow and splayed out 'moustache' style drops and others with more extravagant dips in the centre, aimed at touring cyclists. Cinelli's benchmark shapes and widths set the standard for other manufacturers to follow until the end of the century.

The Giro d'Italia bar is the classic road race bar with a box outline from above, rounded bends and long bar ends usually positioned horizontal to the ground.

The Criterium bar is intended for fast short-circuit racing and has a slightly curved top with shallower drops offering one comfortable position on the hooks.

Classic drop handlebars are still available today, now using the lightest aluminium tubes and even carbon fibre. Classic drop bars tend to feature more rounded constant radius bends, round tubes and more of a box-section appearance from above. Grooves for cables running under the bar tape are the only way they differ from bars produced half a century ago, and that's their undoubted appeal for some.

➔ Classic alloy
road handlebar
and quill stem.

### ➔ Anatomic

Variations on the classic drop handlebar are many and most are designed to offer greater ease of use and comfort to the keen road rider who may not have the flexibility of a pro cyclist. Mostly the intention is to make it easier to ride on the drops.

Anatomic bars tend to interrupt the curve of the hooks with a raised section to bring that part of the bar closer to the rider's hands. On the tops they can have a flattened

← Aero carbon bar with
anatomic drops

section for greater comfort, with the added bonus of presenting a more aero profile.

### ➔ Short

Short drop bars are just that: the smooth curve of the classic bar has a more acute angle, resulting in a tighter bend that raises the height of the drops. This is a more subtle version of the anatomic bar and has become very popular among every type of road rider.

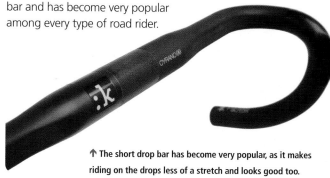

↑ The short drop bar has become very popular, as it makes riding on the drops less of a stretch and looks good too.

### ➔ One-piece

Carbon fibre one-piece bars combine the handlebar and stem in a single construction, clamped to the fork steerer like a standard Aheadset stem. With a fixed position and shape these bars often feature flat aerofoil shaped tops and can save weight over a separate bar and stem assembly. They also cost two or three times more, but for owners of an aero road bike and wheels the small advantage they offer and the looks justify the outlay.

➔ One-piece carbon
aero bars and stem for
top-end road race bikes.

## Handlebar sizing

Apart from their shape and the material used, drop handlebars also come in a range of widths and, generally, two clamping sizes:

Bar widths from 380mm to 460mm in 20mm increments.
Clamping diameter from 26mm for older classic alloy bars to the modern oversize standard 31.8mm or 1¼in.

# Tri-bars

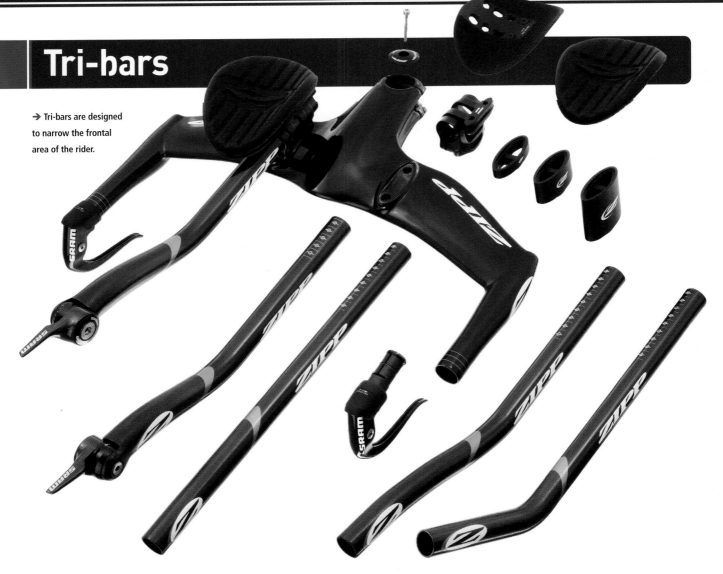

→ Tri-bars are designed to narrow the frontal area of the rider.

A specialist bar for triathlon or time trials, the tri-bar is designed to bring the forearms and hands together in order to reduce the frontal area of the rider. Arm rests support the forearms and twin extension bars placed close together serve as handholds for riders to brace themselves against and steer the machine.

Tri-bars can be bolted on to standard drop handlebars or they may come as a separate or one-piece assembly. Both versions allow the rider to access either the ends of the tops or drops of the bars, or outriggers set to either side of the central bars. This allows the rider to make a starting effort, sit more upright, reach the brakes and control the bike on corners.

Low-profile time trial bikes are designed around the tri-bars on the front end and require careful setting up and time in the saddle to acclimatise the rider to their more extreme riding position. For many road riders the expense and the extra effort required by the riding position of a low-profile bike puts them beyond consideration.

An affordable alternative is a set of bolt-on tri-bars that can be attached to the exposed central section of a pair of standard drop handlebars. These can be fitted for a time trial event and then removed for general riding and are well worth considering if you're an occasional competitor against the watch.

The aerodynamic advantages of the tri-bar are worth multiple seconds per mile depending on the frontal area of the rider. Even at club level time trialling most riders will use some form of tri-bar equipped bike.

← Tri-bars showing arm rests and electronic bar-end gear controls.

# Stems

The threadless stem fitted to an Aheadset is one of the simplest components on the bike, its job being to clamp the handlebars at one end and the fork steerer at the other. Available in 10mm increments, it should be specified according to the rider's preferred reach to the bars. Angled stems can also be flipped to position the bars higher or lower. Alloy is the most popular material used, but titanium and carbon fibre are also available.

→ Spacers can be used below the stem to raise the height of the bars.

← Aheadset stems are usually made from light alloy and come in a range of lengths.

Clamping systems vary but normally there are two pinch bolts for the steerer, with four bolts securing a clamping plate over the front of the bars. If the fork steerer is cut with room for adjustment the threadless stem can be raised or lowered using spacers above or below. Having too many spacers above the stem looks ugly, however, and most bikes have only a few millimetres of available adjustment.

Older bikes with forks using a threaded steerer and traditional headset bearings come with a quill stem. Shaped like an upside down L, the quill stem slots inside the fork steerer and is secured via a long nut pulling on a cone-shaped expander bolt at the bottom of the stem. Since the 1950s quill stems have typically been made from forged aluminium, but in the 1990s steel and titanium were also popular. The advantages of a quill stem are its greater range of vertical adjustment and the ease of achieving this with just one bolt. Some prefer the elegance of the traditional stem, and it's still possible to buy them new from manufacturers keen to appeal to enthusiasts of classic or retro machines.

→ Too many spacers above the stem looks ugly. It's better to distribute them evenly above and below

# Pedals

→ Modern road pedals use a clip-in, click-out binding system.

Pedals are the contact points for the feet and are used to provide a stable platform on which to push. Road pedals for serious cycling are more than just open platforms – they're designed to hold the foot securely in position, or with a small amount of 'float', and allow the rider to concentrate on pedalling without their feet slipping off the pedals.

Since the mid-1980s performance road pedals have been of the 'clipless' or quick-release type. Replacing traditional clips and straps (hence 'clipless'), the breakthrough quick-release pedal was made by ski components company Look and was used by Bernard Hinault to win the 1985 Tour de France. Based on a quick-release ski-binding mechanism, the Look pedal used a triangular plastic plate screwed to the sole of the cycling shoe that locked on to the new pedal using a docking station with a spring-loaded release plate.

In the space of about five years the clipless pedal had rendered the traditional pedal with clips and straps virtually redundant. Today there are half a dozen rival clipless pedals, all different but all offering the same push-to-engage and twist-to-release mode of operation.

## Clips and straps

The original pedal, with toe clips to hold the shoe in position and straps to secure the foot to the pedal, can still be found on budget machines and remains popular with novices learning to pedal faster and harder on a road bike.

There are three elements to a pedal with clips and straps: the pedal, with metal plates front and rear, the front with two screw holes and the rear plates with apertures at both ends; the toe clips, made of metal or plastic, which are screwed into the front

← Look pedals introduced a quick-release system based on a ski binding.

↓ Traditional road pedal with toe clips and straps.

## Quill pedals

**The quill pedal is a traditional alloy road-racing pedal featuring a one-piece back and front plate and a raised quill on the outside. A track pedal is the same but without the quill, for extra clearance on the track banking.**

## Platform

The most basic type of pedal can range from the antique looking rat-trap variety, so-called because of its serrated front and rear plates, to the modern MTB open pedal with a wide flat platform made from aluminium or plastic and sometimes with small sole-gripping studs. Rat-trap style pedals can be uncomfortable if trainers are worn, as the plates start to dig into soft soles. They're also small in area, which makes it even harder for the foot to find a comfortable position.

If you're going to ride platform pedals without toe-clips and straps it's probably best to use the bigger MTB type, which provide a wide and flat area to push on and have studs that will grip a soft-soled shoe. As the pushing element of pedalling is by far the most important part of the pedal stroke it's surprising how far and fast you can ride on this type of pedal.

→ **MTB flat pedals without clips and straps can be surprisingly comfortable and effective, but for serious road riding they're no match for a clipless pedal.**

## Shimano SPD

Though Shimano's popular all-rounder pedal was developed for off-road cycling it also makes an excellent road pedal for general cycling and pretty much everything else, apart from serious sportive riding or racing. Double-sided and with a more open retaining mechanism, the SPD pedal is smaller than a road-only clipless pedal, although a version with a platform surround is also available.

plates; and the straps, made from nylon or leather, which are passed through the holes in the sides of the back plates.

Toe clips and straps can be used with almost any type of shoe, from trainers to traditional touring shoes with little more than a ridged sole. Few people still use traditional leather racing shoes with leather soles on to which plastic or metal cleats have to be nailed. With these the slot in the cleat engaged with the back plate of the pedal, and great care had to be taken to correctly position the cleat when the shoes were new.

It's possible to ride a long way on platform, rat-trap or traditional quill-type pedals without toe clips and straps, especially in flat training shoes. Modern cycling shoes of almost every type, however, have soles designed for the fitment of a cleat to engage with a clipless system and aren't always suitable for riding on a platform pedal without clips and straps. The hard soles of racing shoes will skid off a platform pedal and should only be used with the correct cleat and clipless pedal.

But the good thing about pedals with clips and straps is that they can be used with trainers, and with the straps very loosely tightened are a good way to become accustomed to the feel of having your feet secured to the pedals without the 'locked-in' feel of a clipless system. As a starter pedal or for riding short distances in normal shoes there's still a lot to be said for pedals with toe clips and straps.

↓ **Bikes elegible for Eroica retro events must be fitted with toe clips and straps and have exposed brake cables.**

← **Shimano's SPD pedal is the most versatile clipless pedal, suitable for road or off-road riding.**

↑ **For novice clipless users a pedal like the Click'R makes entry and exit as easy as can be.**

Shimano also produce a novice-friendly version of their SPD pedal called the Click'R. This T400 model comes with a platform surround with a very soft retaining mechanism that makes entry and exit as easy it can be on a clipless pedal. There's also a Shimano multi-release cleat (stamped 'M' or model SM-SH56) that'll release if the foot is pulled sharply upwards as well as by the normal sideway twist of the foot. For many beginners the multi-release cleat offers extra peace of mind, as it'll disengage with a quick reflex reaction.

↑ **The SPD shoe plate is fixed into a recess in the sole by means of two bolts.**

An SPD pedal can be very loosely tensioned via a grub hex screw and this makes entry and exit possible with the minimum of pressure or twisting force. The metal shoe plate is also smaller than a road clipless pedal. Shaped like a cross, it can only be used with SPD-specific shoes that have a recess in the sole into which the shoe plate is fixed with two flat-headed hex screws.

Protecting the shoe plate in a recess in the sole makes walking

← **Casual shoes with SPD shoe plates are ideal for short rides or touring.**

or running much easier, and for that reason SPD shoes are designed for off-road riding and racing, commuting and touring or general riding. Soles aren't as stiff as a dedicated road shoe but don't let that put you off, as a sole with some give can be more comfortable on long rides.

### Shimano SPD-SL

Shimano's SPD-SL is their default road pedal and probably the most popular system with keen road cyclists today. Based on the three-bolt cleat pioneered by Look, the Shimano system works in the same way with a tongue at the apex of the triangular cleat engaging with a tab on the pedal. When the cleat is located in the front of the pedal the rider pushes on the pedal and the broad base of the triangle forces open the spring-loaded plate at the back of the pedal, locking it into place.

Like the off-road version, even budget versions of the SL pedal can be adjusted for spring tension with a grub screw. On the SPD pedal a lightly tensioned spring also allows the foot move freely a few degrees before it disengages from the cleat.

↑ **Shimano's SPD-SL road pedal is the popular choice for many riders.**

On the road SL version the degree of 'float' is determined by the shape of the tongue on the cleat. By changing cleats the user can alter the amount of float from fixed to a few degrees. Three options are available: red is fixed; blue has two degrees of float; yellow has six degrees of float.

↓ **Three shoe-plate designs offer varying degrees of float.**

➔ Time's clipless pedal system allows the foot to move laterally and radially.

↑ Look's Keo pedal is the French brand's evolution of the original clipless pedal.

## Time

Time was the first pedal manufacturer to offer a pedal that allowed the foot to slide laterally as well as offering several degrees of yaw. Their current i-Clic system uses the universal three-bolt sole fixing and allows the foot to move in both directions just like their original pedal design.

## Speedplay

Speedplay has taken an innovative approach to the shoe and pedal system. The problem with the Look/Shimano/Time systems is that they place the sole of the shoe, and thus the foot itself, well above the pedal axle. Speedplay, however, puts the locking mechanism into the cleat itself, which then engages with a very simple, lightweight, lozenge-shaped dock placed directly on the end of the pedal axle. This brings the foot as close to the pedal as possible, creating the most direct drive to the axle. It also means the saddle doesn't have to be raised as it does to compensate for the extra stack height of the other pedal systems.

## Look

Look's latest version of its three-bolt cleat and pedal is called the Keo. Incorporating the same retention system that the French company invented in 1984, the Keo uses a similar-looking triangular cleat to the original Look and the current Shimano version. Tensioning of the retaining plate also differs in that it doesn't use a metal spring but incorporates a flexible plastic or – on the lightweight models – carbon insert which keeps moving parts and weight to a minimum.

➔ Speedplay puts the clipless element into the shoe cleat itself, resulting in the simplest of pedal platforms.

# Replacing cleats

## Cleats

Plastic cleats need to be regularly inspected and replaced from time to time, as walking in them wears the parts which engage with the pedal. Before replacing them, mark the position of the old cleats on the soles of the shoes – this way it'll be easier to fit new ones in the correct positions.

Many pedals allow you to adjust the resistance needed to release the shoe from the pedal via small screws. If the tension screws don't have position markers or an indicator, count the number of clicks or turns when adjusting the first pedal, then repeat the same adjustment with the remaining pedal. This is the best way to achieve the same tension in both pedals.

New cleats bed-in so check the screws after the first few rides. If the cleats come loose it may be difficult, or impossible, to release them from the pedals, which can be dangerous for obvious reasons.

Squeaking cleats are annoying. Unless the root of the problem is wear and tear, it's worth trying a little bearing grease on the tip of the cleat as well as on the rear pedal clamp.

↓ Check shoe plates regularly for excessive wear or damage.

**1** Stand in a relaxed and comfortable position, paying attention to the natural position of your feet, since this is the foot position to aim for when your shoes are engaged with the pedals. Most people, find that their heels point slightly in towards each other and their feet adopt an open 'V' shape with toes pointing slightly outwards.

**2** It's down to personal preference whether you want your feet to be firmly fixed in one position in the pedal or prefer some sideways flexibility (the ability to move your heels). Look offers cleats featuring 0° (black), 4.5° (grey) and 9° (red) of heel movement. Shimano also offers a fixed version (red) and a flexible one (yellow). Time cleats all have a degree of flexibility built in.

**3** When fitting cleats, always ensure that each cleat sits flush with the curvature of the sole of the shoe. If there's a gap between the sole and the cleat, the cleat may deform in use, which can cause problems engaging and releasing from the pedal.

**4** Lay the main body of the cleat in position on the sole of the shoe, then fit the screw plates, making sure that they're positioned to allow the screws to fit easily and engage with the threads in the shoes. Tighten the screws two or three turns – ideally using your fingers. The screws should provide no resistance during this process.

**5** Initially, position the cleat so that the securing screws are in the middle of the elongated holes in the screw plates. Use a set square positioned against the rear edge of the cleat so that you can clearly see the angle of the

cleat relative to the shoe. Adjust this angle to suit your own preference, bearing in mind your natural foot position when standing, as mentioned previously.

**6** If you ride with your heels turned heavily inwards, you should position the shoe towards the outside of the pedal in the area where the ball of the foot is. This gives more flexibility for the heel. Therefore in this case the cleats should be positioned towards the inside edge of the shoe. When you're happy that the cleats are correctly positioned, progressively tighten the screws, ideally to the specified torque.

**7** Once all the cleat screws are tight, working on each pedal in turn, lock your shoe into the pedal and check that neither your heel nor your ankle make contact with the pedal crank.

**8** Check that your foot position is comfortable, and also make sure that the ball of your foot is in a central position above the pedal axle. It's better to place the axle a little behind the ball of the foot than in front, where it places more stress on the Achilles and calves. If adjustment is required, loosen the cleat once again and realign as necessary.

**9** In order to check that the cleat position is the same for both shoes, hold the shoes against each other, as shown. When the cleats align with each other the shoe heels should meet exactly.

# Seatpost

Two functions are performed by a bike's seatpost: supporting the saddle with a clamp at the top; and being long enough to be adjusted up or down the seat tube to alter the height of the saddle.

Ever since the invention of the safety bicycle with standard-sized wheels, pretty much the only way to determine the correct height of the saddle in relation to the pedals has been by sliding the seatpost up or down the seat tube and then securing it with a small clamp at the top of the tube. However, as seat tube angles have become steeper on modern-era machines, improved seatpost design has allowed the saddle to sit above the post rather than canted forward to place the rider's knees closer to a vertical line drawn from the bottom bracket.

→ A standard seatpost slides up and down the seat tube and is secured with a single-bolt clamp.

Clamping the saddle on a modern seatpost is usually done via a single bolt which passes through the neck of the post and pulls down on a separate H-shaped piece with channels either side that engage with the rails of the saddle. A second, identically shaped piece sits below the rails in a U-shaped moulding that can be grooved or smooth.

With the bolt undone but still in place the saddle and clamps can be slid a few centimetres fore and aft along the rails as well as adjusted for pitch. A twin-bolt clamp normally has one bolt to micro-adjust the pitch of the saddle while the other clamps it tightly in place.

It can be fiddly to fit a new saddle, as the two loose clamps have to be carefully positioned directly above the hole in the neck of the seatpost before the bolt is inserted and gently turned until the threads on the upper clamping plate are engaged. Once that's been achieved it's

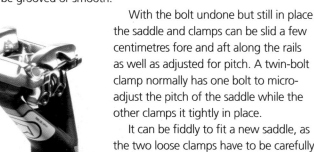

← The seat is secured to the seatpost with two H-shaped clamping plates.

a relatively simple case of adjusting the saddle in both orientations before tightening the bolt to the correct torque setting.

A seatpost can be adjusted up and down; it will also allow the saddle to be shifted back and forth between limits marked on the saddle rails. The pitch of the saddle can be determined too. There's one more way to play with the fit and that's with the layback of the post itself or, more commonly, the neck of the seatpost. Some posts have a kink in them to allow the rider to sit further behind or over the bottom bracket. An extended neck at the top of the seatpost does the same thing, more elegantly some would say.

← Some seatposts are angled to position the saddle further behind or over the bottom bracket.

## Seatpost diameters

The standard diameter for a road bike seatpost is 27.2mm or 1in, but oversized frames may take a seatpost with a 27.4mm or bigger, going up in 2mm increments. Before you change your seatpost check the diameter of the old one – it should be etched into the material towards the bottom of the post.

## Seatpost types

Aluminium is the most popular material for seatposts and it remains hard to beat in terms of lightness, strength and ease of forging. The neck can be forged as part of the tube itself or it can be a separate piece pressed into the tube. An aluminium seatpost can be very light, and with various anodised finishes can complement the appearance of any machine.

Carbon-fibre seatposts have gained in popularity, not so much thanks to the small reductions in weight over aluminium but due to the desirability of the material and, more significantly, the vibration-damping offered in longer versions. The design is similar to aluminium with either a one-piece post and neck or a carbon post with aluminium or carbon neck inserted into the post. The clamps can be carbon or aluminium.

Long 'tuned' carbon seatposts can be specified in carbon frames, especially compact or sloping top tube types, which provide more than the usual amount of flex. In effect the seatpost itself acts as a micro suspension unit absorbing vibes from the road and flexing under the weight of the rider.

→ Carbon-fibre seatposts can offer a degree of damping, especially in a carbon frame.

# Saddle

Of all the points of contact on a bike the saddle is the one that can provide the most discomfort. Hands on bars and feet in shoes rarely cause problems that can't be alleviated relatively easily, but the saddle of a bicycle can be a notoriously irksome and fickle device.

Even when you think you may have found the perfect saddle it can quickly remind you, especially after some time away from riding, that it's the one bike part that wasn't made in heaven. In extreme cases the wrong saddle can bruise and chafe the user – enough to put the occasional rider off serious cycling for good. That said, the right saddle can be a wonderful piece of kit, with looks to complement the bike and, considering the minimalism of the modern saddle, amazing all-day comfort and support.

## Shape

Sleek and narrow need not spell discomfort. In fact, ill-fitting saddles with more generous proportions and excess padding can be much less comfortable than a correctly fitted lightweight racing saddle.

A typical road saddle has a long narrow nose with a gently flared rear, but within those parameters there are endless permutations of shape and profile. Some may be little more than attempts to create a distinctive or stylish look, but many are genuinely designed to provide a more anatomically comfortable platform than the competition.

Many models come in a range of, typically, three sizes that usually correspond to the width of the rider's sit bones. Some brands, like Specialized for instance, offer saddle-fitting services that can match riders to correct sizes of their appropriate saddles.

## Materials

Leather was the material used in early saddles, but while there remain devotees of the famous Brooks B17 all-leather saddle most cyclists aren't prepared to put in the 100 miles of agony required to break-in a modern version of the Brooks. Nor is breaking-in the only downside of a leather saddle – the weight of

↑ An uncomfortable saddle can blight a long ride.

← A typical modern road saddle looks stylish and narrow.

→ Saddle-fit systems like the Specialized Body Geometry system are well worth considering.

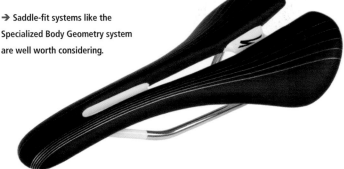

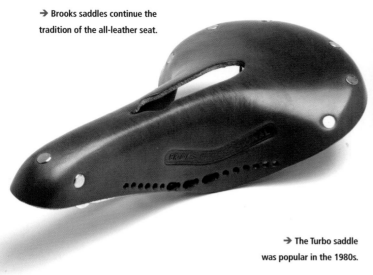

→ Brooks saddles continue the
tradition of the all-leather seat.

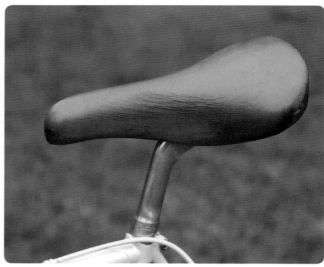

→ The Turbo saddle
was popular in the 1980s.

leather and its dislike of a soaking are additional drawbacks. But a modern leather saddle, treated to repel water and using lighter rails and plates on to which the leather is riveted, can just about be justified for stylish and leisurely road riding.

Since the 1970s performance road saddles have featured a plastic-moulded base covered with a layer of padding and a thin leather or plasticised skin stretched over the top and either glued or stapled to the inside lip of the base.

During the 1980s the affordable, comfortable and attractive racing saddle came of age with models like Selle Italia's Turbo, used by Tour de France winners and club cyclists alike. Then at the turn of the 21st century more exotic materials, like titanium and carbon fibre, began to appear as attention turned to reducing weight on the latest generation of lightweight aluminium and carbon bikes.

## Padding and cut-outs

Most riders would put comfort at least on a par with looks when it comes to saddle choice. After the shape of the saddle, and

how it fits the individual's anatomy, padding comes second but is nevertheless an important factor in determining levels of comfort and vibration absorption.

Thicker and plusher doesn't necessarily equal greater levels of comfort. More important is how the padding works when in contact with the sit bones and perineum. The vexed issue of penile numbness in men can be affected by the padding in the centre of the saddle, but other factors like saddle angle and the saddle shape or surface contours are just as important. To combat penile numbness the trend is for a channel down the centre of the saddle or even a cut-out section.

When considering saddle comfort it's important to take into account all of the above points, and not elevate one above the others. Don't forget that there's additional padding in the seat of

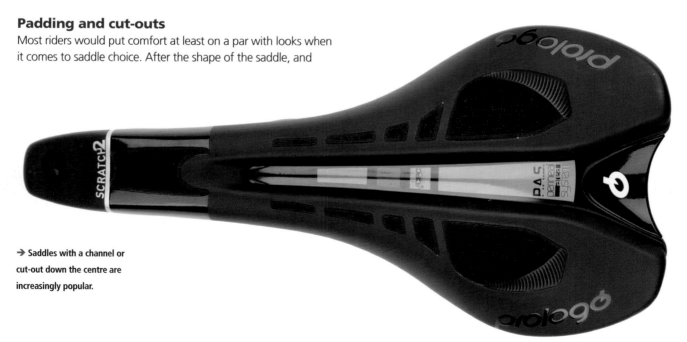

→ Saddles with a channel or
cut-out down the centre are
increasingly popular.

→ Women are more sensitive to
saddle choice than men.

a pair of cycling shorts, and how your shorts feel on the saddle
should also be taken into account. Also, while it may be tempting
to buy the same saddle as a Tour de France rider it's worth noting
that professional stage racers can weigh one third less than a
hobby cyclist. They also wear the highest-tech cycling shorts and
push a lot harder on the pedals, thus reducing even further their
reliance on the padding in their saddle.

## Saddles for women

Women's greater sensitivity to saddles has resulted in designs and
innovations that have led to saddles with quite distinct differences
to conventional models. That isn't to say that a conventional
saddle won't suit a woman's anatomy, as, like any cyclist, a range
of factors from saddle shape to its orientation on the seatpost,
the weight of the rider, and even the type of the padding in the
rider's shorts, can all affect saddle comfort.

A female-specific saddle will typically be wider at the back to
align with female sit bones and may have a shorter nose in an
attempt to reduce genital numbness. Wider and shorter aren't
necessarily the answer, however, as reducing pressure in one area
can just shift it to another part of the saddle.

One of the most radical solutions is the fork-nosed saddle,
with the ISM Adamo model featuring two stubby nose pieces
and an angular padded rear. Other cut-out designs with a central
piece removed from the middle of the saddle are also favoured by
some female and male riders.

For women cyclists it's even more important to either search
out a saddle-fitting service or at least find a retailer who'll allow
tests rides on a variety of saddle types.

→ Some radically shaped saddles
have been a big hit with female
riders.

# CHAPTER 4
# CLOTHING AND ACCESSORIES

There's an amazing amount of bike clothing for every season and discipline. And because cycling is such a specialist sport few, if any, items of cycle clothing pass for 'civilian' – an undershirt, maybe, or possibly one of the less shouty sock designs. Just about all riding gear, from shoes, to shorts, gloves, tops and helmets, is cycling specific. You can try to kit yourself out with non-cycling attire, but if you want to ride comfortably for more than half-an-hour, nothing beats the real thing. But putting together, in one go, a year's worth of cycling clothing is a big ask financially. For new riders it's best to start with an outfit suitable for the current season, then add to the collection as the year progresses.

There are many versatile pieces which can be used throughout the seasons, and with a few of these it's possible to keep costs down with one or two additional layers as and when the seasons demand it. As with many aspects of cycling, it pays to observe how experienced riders dress and not be shy to ask for their advice.

← Shorts and a summer jersey can be added to as the seasons unfold.

# Price and fit

↑ Cycling takes place in all weather conditions and is hard on clothing.

Budget cycling clothing can be perfectly serviceable but will almost certainly wear out faster than higher-priced quality kit created from lighter technical fabrics. Serious cycling takes place in all conditions and makes big demands on kit which has to repel the elements, protect the contact points and provide crash protection – all while the rider pedals along without overheating, freezing or drowning in perspiration. Not surprisingly the brands which have cracked all or most of these demands command reassuringly high prices for their cycling collections.

Ensuring that the clothing fits properly adds another dilemma to the new rider and to cyclists buying online. It's very important to get correct-sized items to ensure a comfortably snug fit that doesn't restrict but won't flap around, causing unnecessary drag on the rider.

A shop with expert assistance is the best place to try on cycling clothing; if that isn't possible, careful use of sizing charts can work online. Sizing among clothing brands can be notoriously inconsistent, with big differences especially between European and American manufacturers. A small 'S' Italian climbing specialist may not have the same dimensions as a small 'S' American weekend rider.

Cycling's increasing popularity has resulted in much greater choice when it comes to clothing and accessories. As more women take up road cycling there's been a corresponding mini-boom in clothing for women, with features, tailoring and styles which mean that – at last – female cyclists can now look well beyond XS male clothing.

→ Women have a much greater choice in female-specific cycle clothing.

# Shorts

→ Bib shorts are the most popular style of cycling shorts.

Shorts are the most important item of bike clothing as well as the most misunderstood, especially among non-cyclists. Lycra cycling shorts are designed to be light, to fit snugly but move freely through the pedalling action. They need to grip the mid thigh without riding up and preferably cover the upper back, usually with a bib-style cut. Most importantly a cycling short has a padded insert that insulates the rider from the saddle, providing much-needed comfort, and a shaped seating area that won't chafe or ride up. The first rule of cycling shorts is that you wear them with nothing on underneath, as the padded insert is designed to sit directly next to the skin.

Although a bib-type short is the most popular, it's possible to buy conventional non-bib style Lycra cycling shorts which can be perfectly comfortable and effective. If used with clip-on braces they won't slip down at the back either, but most riders prefer the bib style as it stays up, offering lots of room to tuck in an undervest and some welcome warmth to the kidney area of the lower back.

Standard bib shorts aren't always favoured by women, who have to strip off if they want to pee, but there are female-friendly bib shorts with a variety of clips, halter necks and zips which enable the user to take a comfort break with a lot less undressing.

A quality pair of shorts can be one of the most expensive items of clothing, which can be baffling when one pair of black cycling shorts looks much like another. But experienced road cyclists know that budget cycling shorts can be a false economy – wearing out quickly, riding up and having a thin insert, they can spoil many a long ride. That's not to say that keenly priced shorts won't suit you, as saddle choice and orientation, road conditions and individual preferences all play their part in this very personal aspect of cycling.

Up close the differences between a premium pair of cycling shorts and a budget version is obvious. Thicker quality Lycra, more than six panels (which indicate a more tailored fit), mesh

## Why chamois?

Traditional cycling shorts used to have a single piece of soft chamois leather stitched into their saddle area. There was no padding in them, but pre-Lycra shorts were made of wool, which at least provided a small amount of insulation from the saddle. Later versions of the 'chammy' in Lycra shorts were padded, but today synthetic fabrics – which are easier to wash and dry faster – have replaced the chammy in all but the most retro classic shorts.

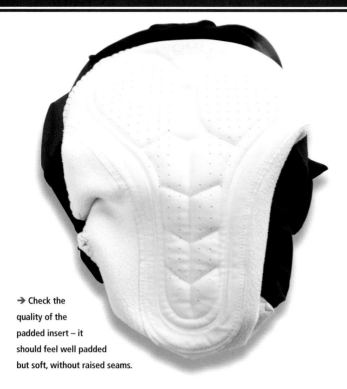

→ Check the quality of the padded insert – it should feel well padded but soft, without raised seams.

or breathable material in the bib and silicone grippers all indicate that care and attention has been applied to the fit and finish.

Again, the quality of the padded insert should be obvious. Turn the shorts inside out and feel the material in the pad and how the padding compresses. It must be said, however, that it isn't until you've worn a pair of shorts on a decent ride that you will know if that particular short and insert suits your shape. Some use a branded seat insert and if that insert agrees with you it's something to look out for when buying other shorts in the future.

## Baggies

Mountain bikers often wear long, hardwearing, baggy shorts, which also tend to be favoured by downhillers and freeriders who don't spend hours pedalling in the saddle. Cross-country mountain bike racers wear conventional skin shorts, but it's quite possible to wear baggies for long rides in comfort if you find a pair that agree with you or if you wear a pair of skin shorts or padded liners underneath.

Padded liners are tight-fitting briefs with a padded insert. MTB baggies have padded inserts or at least a towelling liner which can sit directly next to the skin, but there'll always be more movement around the saddle area – especially for men – and some bunching with baggy shorts. Even a small amount of bunched material in the saddle area can cause discomfort and chafing on longer rides.

For touring, a pair of loose-fitting shorts can be worn over skin shorts and the look is agreeably non-competitive. It's worth trying out the shorts combination to get the length correct and to check that they don't ride up the leg or restrict pedalling. Baggy shorts with flat seams in the saddle area are also less likely to be felt through the padded insert of the skin shorts.

↑ Baggy shorts can be worn for general road cycling or touring.

# Base layers

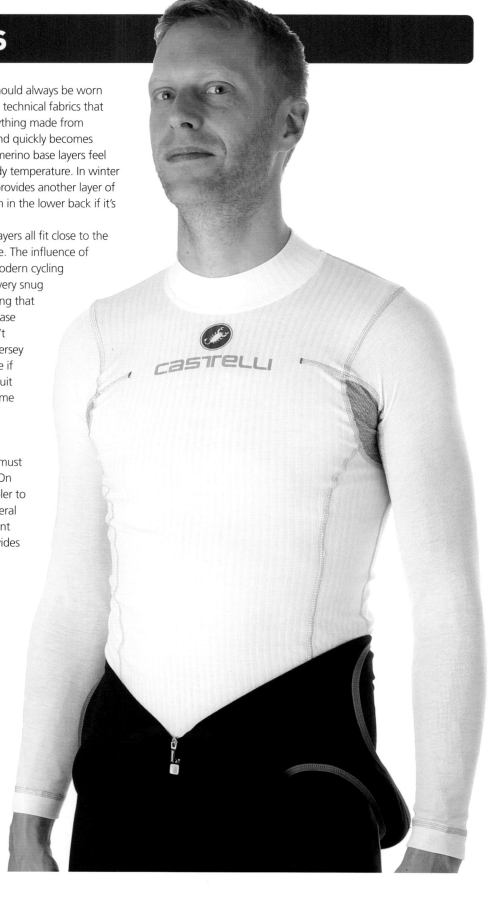

A base layer, short- or long-sleeved, should always be worn on all but the hottest of days. Stretchy technical fabrics that wick away sweat are preferable to anything made from cotton, which soaks up perspiration and quickly becomes clammy and misshapen. Lightweight merino base layers feel great and have a neutral effect on body temperature. In winter a thicker base layer with a high neck provides another layer of insulation, and some welcome warmth in the lower back if it's cut with a longer tail for cycling.

It's worth ensuring that your base layers all fit close to the body with as little bunching as possible. The influence of aerodynamics in cycling means that modern cycling jerseys and jackets are designed for a very snug fit with no bunched material or anything that can flap in the wind. A tightly fitting base layer, especially around the arms, won't compromise the fit of a performance jersey or jacket. That'll be even more the case if you're wearing a one-piece Lycra skinsuit or skin-tight, short-sleeved jersey for time trialling or fast road rides.

Those are the only times when it's possible to exclude a base layer, when every second counts and the clothing must perform at its lightest and most aero. On very hot days it may also be a little cooler to wear just a thin road jersey, but in general it's best to always wear one. In the event of a sliding crash a base layer also provides a small amount of extra protection against abrasions.

→ **A tight-fitting base layer should always be worn under a cycling top.**

# Jerseys

→ There's an infinite choice of colours and designs when it comes to cycling jerseys.

A short-sleeved cycling jersey holds out the promise of summer rides, the exhilaration of racing, sitting outside cafes in the sunshine and the Tour de France. After the bike, a short-sleeved cycling top says more about you than any other item or accessory.

Unless you're a dyed-in-the-wool club cyclist who insists on showing your loyalty in club colours, there's an endless choice of hues, patterns and pro team strips to choose from. You can play safe in black or a plain colour, or telegraph your allegiance to a favourite pro team, rider, charity or even the yeast extract you spread on your toast! It's fun to choose all types of cycling tops – the only problem is where to keep them all.

As with all items of cycling clothing, function and fabric technology are the drivers behind the evolution of a top that has several important jobs to do. Most obviously a cycling top should be light in weight and close-fitting enough not to flap in the wind. It needs to be tailored with a longer body than a T-shirt or rugby top to stop it riding up and to cover the lower back when the rider's stretched out on the bike.

This is less important when bib shorts are worn as then the fabric from the shorts covers the lower back, but that can make it very difficult to reach the pockets, which is another unique aspect of the cycling top. Most have two or three pockets along the lower back, which can be accessed while the rider is on the bike. Mostly these are used for small items of food, like energy bars and gels, but the pockets can also be used for essential items like a mobile phone and wallet, multi-tool, spare tubes, tyre levers and a thin rain top.

If the pockets are too high on the back it can be very frustrating trying to access them, both on and off the bike, so it's always worth trying on a top if you like to fill the back pockets with stuff. Numerous tops now come with small additional zipped security pouches for mobile phones and keys.

↓ Make sure you can reach the pockets in the back of the jersey.

← Lightweight summer jerseys often come with a full-length zip for greater ventilation.

Sleeves and hems on cycling jerseys should either be elasticated or at least be a snug enough fit not to ride up or flap loosely around the arms or midriff. Zips can be full or neck-length, and the quality of the zip is often an indication of the quality of the rest of the top. Plastic branded zips like YKK are preferable to metal ones, especially if you have sensitive skin, and there are now jerseys available with slider and water resistant zips. Full-length zipped short-sleeve jerseys are favoured for summer riding, when they can be unzipped part or all of the way down for maximum ventilation.

Many and varied are the fabrics available for jerseys, ranging from wool to the most sophisticated water-repellent and lightweight breathable fabrics. The traditional cycling jersey is made from fine wool, and modern versions have evolved the wool jersey into an extremely comfortable and well-fitted garment, though they can be pricey. Wool shouldn't be dismissed as old-fashioned, as a lighter-weight modern wool top is very good at wicking away perspiration, is snug but not stuffy, feels great and often looks good too.

At the other end of the scale a 100% acrylic jersey of the type that's been worn by club cyclists for decades won't perform anywhere near as well as a woollen or modern wicking fabric jersey, but as a budget option it'll pass muster better than a non-cycling-specific top.

At professional level the search for low-drag clothing has led to cycling jerseys that fit and look like the all-Lycra skinsuits used for time trialling. Material technology allows for tops of gossamer thin, body-hugging material that can be worn all day and save enough precious Watts of energy to make the difference between first and second place.

↓ Modern wool jerseys are very comfortable and stylish.

→ Figure hugging racing tops are almost as aero as a one-piece skinsuit.

## Short-sleeve rain jersey

Castelli's Perfetto short-sleeve jersey is a lightweight, racing-ready version of the severe weather Gabba jacket. Intended for hard riding in wet and chilly conditions, the Perfetto features a lighter weight version of Gore's Winsdstopper fabric on the front with a water repelling, breathable fabric on the back. A longer tail-piece protects the backside from water sprayed up from the back wheel and the jersey has a versatile full zip and three back pockets. Worn with water repelling arm warmers, jerseys like this are ideal for serious riding in wet weather, whatever the season.

These jerseys have rear pockets and zips in the conventional style but should only be worn in hot weather, for sportives or racing. High prices for such tops will put many people off anyway. Others may balk at an item of clothing that leaves little to the imagination and can be almost see-through. There are many high quality technical tops that offer more practical all-day properties yet still fit snugly without making the wearer look like a Wall's banger.

A short-sleeved top can be worn with arm-hugging Lycra or Lycra-mix arm warmers, with the added bonus of being able to remove the arm warmers and fold them into the back pockets when the temperature goes up. Long sleeves are also harder to tailor for a tight fit without being a struggle to get into. That's possibly why the long-sleeved cycling jersey with a short zip has fallen out of favour, replaced by full-zip lightweight jackets, breathable soft shell tops and arm warmers.

↓ Arm warmers are a versatile way to keep the chill off.

# Socks

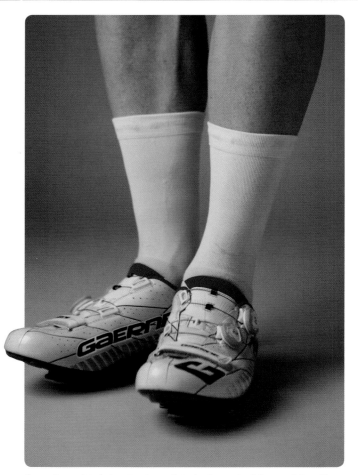

↑ A cycling sock is designed to fit snugly in the shoe and tightly around the ankles.

↑ High or low? It's up to you – don't let the 'style police' decide that one.

There are socks and there are cycling socks, and never the twain shall meet! Every effort to dress in the appropriate cycling clothing is negated by the addition of a pair of civilian socks. Too long, too short, baggy, the wrong colour – all are taboo among the fraternity of road cyclists who live by a long list of esoteric codes, several of which refer to socks. Notwithstanding the cycling 'style police', there are good reasons why cycling-specific socks not only make sense, but look great too.

A cycling sock should be thin and stretchy enough to fit snugly inside a road cycling shoe. If the sock is too thick or baggy on the foot it can move about in the shoe, reducing pedalling efficiency and power. On a long ride an ill-fitting sock can become uncomfortable and irritating, especially if it's ribbed or has raised seams. A cycling sock works like a thin liner inside a well-fitted shoe, smoothing out imperfections with the minimum of bulk or insulation. A thin sock is especially important when riding in the summer, when the ambient temperature and heat from the road can make it feel like your feet are baking in your shoes.

Above the shoe, a cycling sock has one function – to grip the ankle or lower leg tightly enough to prevent the sock slipping down. Most cycling socks have an elasticated upper gripper band a few centimetres deep, which once pulled up won't move for the duration of a ride.

It has to be said that a neatly worn cycling sock complements a cycling shoe in a way that a saggy office version in beige sadly doesn't. Lively is the debate among the style-conscious as to the correct length of a cycling sock: traditionalists advocate light colours and no more than ankle height; rebels favour every hue and up to just below the calf. Rise above it folks – both types have their merits.

In winter a thicker sock can be worn purely for the warmth, especially if worn inside a slightly bigger winter shoe or under overshoes. It can be longer too, as it'll often be worn under winter cycling tights or leg warmers that cover the ankle. There are cycling-specific winter socks, some made from wool or merino wool, but it's also possible to wear tight-fitting general sports socks at this time of year.

# Shoes

The cycling shoe is basically a foot-shaped component of the pedal. Its primary role is to hold the foot securely on the pedal, allowing the leg to transmit maximum power through the cranks with a minimum of flex. The sole must be stiff and the upper often has multiple closure systems to ensure that the foot's held comfortably but immovably inside the shoe itself.

Materials used in the construction of a cycling shoe need to be robust enough to perform in all conditions without losing their shape or falling apart. Depending on how much walking you intend to do there are cycling shoes which are designed with lugged rubber soles with some flex in them, which feel like a stiff work shoe, through to rock-hard, carbon-soled racing shoes with little more than thin plastic buffers to prevent the shoe pitching you on your behind as you make your way between team bus and bike. Take a look at a professional rider trying to walk up the steps at the signing-on ceremony of a race and you'll see how impractical a racing shoe can be for anything other than pedalling.

← Shoes for road cycling with stiff soles aren't made for walking in.

## Road shoe types

The sole of a cycling shoe tells you all you need to know about its intended use. A smooth all-carbon or composite sole with minimal compromises for walking is for racing and competition.

↓ Road shoes have hard plastic or composite soles with the universal multi-bolt fixing system.

A smooth hard plastic or carbon composite sole with walking buffers represents the bulk of road shoe designs, offering a stiff but not completely unyielding platform. Both types will have the industry standard three-bolt threaded inserts compatible with most road-biased shoe plate and pedal systems.

## MTB/all-rounder shoe

Rubber soles with grippy ridges or lugs and even studs (for cyclo-cross racing), and a recessed two-bolt fixing system for Shimano SPD shoe plates, are intended for leisure riding, commuting and training. This style of shoe shouldn't be discounted by road cyclists, as these cyclo-cross/MTB/touring shoes are comfortable and versatile. Premium versions, designed for cyclo-cross or MTB racing, are almost as stiff as a competition road shoe, albeit slightly heavier and chunkier.

A road shoe upper can take many forms, some of them not unlike an all-terrain walking shoe (MTB/road) while at the extreme performance end the upper can be little more than an almond-shaped carbon shell. Style plays its part too, and nowhere is that more apparent than the eye-watering range of colourways favoured by some brands, which, contrary to the

→ An MTB shoe is worth considering for training, commuting or touring.

↑ Closure systems may include Velcro and a wire system like the Boa.

↓ Some road shoes now come with traditional laces to hold the foot in place.

sober habits of many road cyclists, find some enthusiasts quite happy to flaunt a pair of pearlescent white shoes.

High on the list of practical considerations are the stiffness of the sole, the shoe's overall weight and the quality and type of closure system on the upper. Most road cyclists will choose a mid-level road shoe that has a synthetic lightweight upper, very likely with mesh panels for ventilation. The closure system can be by two or three Velcro straps, a combination of Velcro and a ratchet strap or the dial-and-wire 'Boa' branded system.

Traditional lace-ups have also made a niche comeback and been used at the highest level, and while some might question the efficiency of laces it demonstrates that the main job of the closure system is to hold the foot securely and comfortably on the pedal. The notion that the foot must be clamped in place to allow the rider to pull up on the pedals is mistaken, as in practice little or no effort is put into 'pulling up' on the pedals.

Most road shoes are designed for riding in warm, dry weather and have no insulation and a minimum of padding around the entry and tongue. Vents and mesh panels are the only ways to keep the feet cool, and although water will run out of vents and drain holes the only way to properly insulate or waterproof a pair of road shoes is to wear overshoes of various materials and weights for summer and winter conditions.

A pair of road shoes can be used all year round if overshoes are pulled over them in wet or cold conditions (see winter accessories below). Thinner shoe covers made from Lycra or a waterproofed material can be used to protect the shoes on cooler days in summer or when it's very wet.

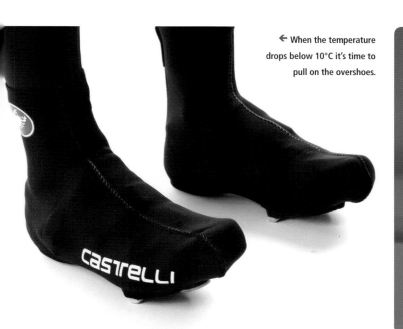

← When the temperature drops below 10°C it's time to pull on the overshoes.

## Toe covers

Neoprene shoe covers that fit over the toe or up to halfway up the shoe can be effective on cool spring or autumn rides, especially if worn over well-vented shoes. They keep the toes warm and block draughts as well as keeping road grime off the shoe. Little more than a purse-shaped pouch, they're inexpensive and can easily be carried in the back pocket of a cycling top.

↑ Toe covers can keep the chill off in spring and autumn.

## Overshoes

Overshoes keep the feet warm and dry and are an essential accessory. Throughout the year there are occasions when it'll be necessary to wear overshoes and at least one pair should be in every cyclist's kit bag. Overshoes' primary function is to insulate the foot from cold temperatures, which particularly affect the feet (and hands) when the mercury drops below 10°C.

Road shoes intended for dry and warm riding are ill-equipped to deal with cold weather, with vents and mesh panels chilling the feet to uncomfortable and sometimes numbing levels. There are few more disagreeable sensations than freezing feet on a winter ride.

Typically overshoes are made from thin neoprene that stretches tightly over the shoe and covers the ankle. The insulating effect of the neoprene keeps the feet warm and water is also repelled. A road overshoe will have a cut-out on the sole for the shoe plate to poke through and will be secured at the back with a zip or Velcro.

If MTB shoes are used with a recessed shoe plate and chunkier sole it's better to use an MTB overshoe, which has a cut-out that extends the length of the shoe, exposing the sole of the shoe completely. This allows the recessed shoe plates to engage more easily with the pedal and enables the user to walk in the overshoe.

Most types of overshoe

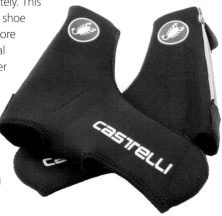

→ Overshoes are an inexpensive but essential road shoe accessory.

also have reinforced toe and heel pads for walking, which needs to be undertaken carefully as it's easy to scuff or damage a thin overshoe. Neoprene is the default material but lighter, breathable overshoes using Gore-Tex and rain-repelling materials can be equally as effective.

A well-fitted overshoe can be a struggle to pull on over the shoe, and the whole process has to be carried out carefully to avoid ripping the shoe-plate hole, popping a seam or breaking a zip. They come in sizes that relate to your road shoe and it's essential to get overshoes that are neither too tight nor baggy.

Alternatives to traditional overshoes are oversocks, which are just that – socks which pull over the shoe, cover the ankle and keep the feet warm in dry but cool conditions. Few riders these days cut shoe-plate holes in a pair of street socks, as numerous brands offer reinforced fabric oversocks with shoe-plate holes. Thinner shoe covers are also popular for summer riding and time trialling as they offer an aerodynamic advantage, keep chilly breezes out and keep the shoes pristine.

↓ Thin shoe covers protect the shoes and offer a small aerodynamic advantage.

# Helmets

Wearing a cycling helmet is mandatory in some countries and in all sanctioned competition or challenge events, from road racing to sportives and triathlon. Even in countries where helmets aren't compulsory most road cyclists choose to wear one as a matter of course. Manufacturers have responded to the rocketing demand for cycle helmets by producing a crash hat for every occasion.

Helmets can be distinguished by their relative weights, adjustability, quality of materials, vents and aerodynamics. These are all relatively important features that persuade many riders to purchase helmets in the upper price bands, but the fact remains that most helmets are constructed in the same way from a polystyrene mould with a thin hardshell cover.

A mid-priced road helmet should weigh less than 250gm and have a padded cradle inside the helmet with at least one dial or ratchet for adjustment. It'll be vented to allow air to flow thorough the helmet but won't necessarily have any aerodynamic features. Fixing straps will be nylon, adjustable with a buckle and secured with a snap clip. Additional pads should come with the helmet and can be used to fine-tune the fit inside the shell itself, especially around the forehead where sweat and shell shape have the greatest effect on comfort and fit.

Although internal adjustable cradles make this less critical, it's always worth trying a range of different helmet brands to

↑ Wearing a helmet is compulsory for sportive events and racing.

find the moulded shell shape that suits your head best. Even in the correct size a helmet that doesn't conform to the shape of a rider's head will never feel quite right.

↓ Most helmets have an adjustable internal cradle with soft padded strips for comfort.

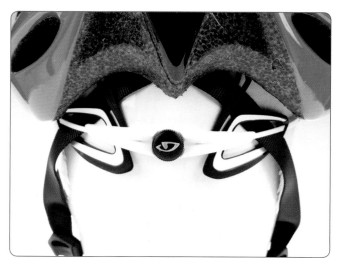

→ Great ventilation, low weight
and snazzy colours distinguish a top-end helmet.

## Top-end helmets

Racing determines the features on helmets at the premium end, with lightness, ventilation and aerodynamics all driven by the demands of the pro racing cyclists who are paid to wear them. There's no doubt that the sleek looks and finishes of the most expensive helmets persuade many of us to part with the extra cash, but they offer no more safety than any other certified helmet.

A very light helmet is worth paying more for and effective ventilation can make cycling in high temperatures – especially on mountain passes – more bearable than in a low-vent helmet. In that sense an unobtrusive, well-fitted, breezily ventilated and light helmet is safer than one that irks the wearer with its poor fit, lack of vents and head-squeezing shape and weight.

Aerodynamic helmets have been commonplace in time trialling for some time, but in recent years the aero road helmet has taken the concept and adapted it for racing and even everyday road cycling. Gone is the long tail and bullet-like unvented shell of the most extreme versions of the TT helmet. The aero road helmet has a similar lack of vents – though it may have one or two – and a much shorter teardrop shape, but wind tunnel tests have shown that these helmets create less drag than conventional shell shapes with multiple vents.

Some venting has been introduced to aero helmets and

professional cyclists have shown that they can be raced in all day, but for the non-professional the trade-off between saving a few seconds per kilometre and a cooler head may not be worth the premium prices that aero road helmets command.

↓ Aero road helmets are less obviously vented but can save a few seconds per kilometre.

# Gloves

← Summer cycling gloves perform several useful functions.

Cycling gloves perform four functions: they keep the hands warm; protect them in the event of a crash; absorb unwelcome vibes from the bars; and help the rider grip the bars.

Their most obvious function is the first one, and for several months of the year a pair of warm gloves are essential in most northern climes. Full-fingered cycling gloves are less bulky than skiing gloves and should be a snug fit to prevent the hands moving around inside them when gripping the bars or riding out of the saddle with hands on the hoods.

Even the thickest cycling-specific winter gloves should be dextrous enough to operate the gears and brakes, pull something from the back pockets and work a zip or two. In spring and autumn thinner gloves will suffice, and it's even possible to wear non-cycling-specific gloves as long they're tight fitting. Everyday winter gloves won't have crash protection on the palms, nor will they have adjustable cuffs or use material designed to grip the bars and work the levers. And they definitely won't have a patch of towelling along the forefinger for wiping away sweat and snot!

Summer road cycling gloves, also known as cycling mitts, are worn to protect the hands from jarring and to allow the rider to maintain a secure grip on the bars and levers. They're always fingerless and made from the lightest materials, often with Lycra on the backs. The palms can be thin leather or a grippy synthetic material over a thin layer of padding. Gloves with a gel insert offer extra damping from vibration for riders who suffer from sore hands.

Cycling mitts can be worn quite comfortably in hot weather and they do a good job soaking up sweat from the hands, while the palm of the glove prevents the hands from slipping on brake levers when riding out of the saddle. In the event of a crash mitts protect the palms from nasty and painful grazing. Riding with grazed hands is very painful and explains why most professional cyclists wear mitts to ensure that – however covered in blood they are – they can still remount and continue racing.

↓ Winter cycling gloves have to be well insulated but still allow the wearer to work the controls.

# Jackets

→ A cycling jacket is an essential piece of clothing in cooler conditions.

A jacket is one of the most versatile pieces of clothing in the cyclist's wardrobe. Long-sleeved with a full-length zip and with pockets at the back, there's a jacket for everything but high summer riding in a wide range of price points.

Cold-weather cycling is what most jackets are designed for, and in the higher price bands lightweight, windproof but breathable materials make them well worth the extra cost. Some may have shower proofing too, with waterproof zips and secure pockets.

A zipped or buttoned high collar keeps the neck warm while cuffs and hems are elasticated to keep the wind out. The correct-size cycling jacket should be a snug fit but not necessarily as tight as a short-sleeve cycling jersey, as the jacket should be roomy enough to be worn with an extra layer or two underneath and should be comfortable though not restricting. Some of the highest quality jackets using the latest thermal fabrics, however, are amazingly warm and can be worn with little more than a base layer in sub-10°C temperatures.

Budget jackets may not boast high-tech fabrics but are perfectly effective in cold weather as long as the rider is wearing a wicking base layer. They can be bulkier to wear, the fit may not be as tailored and cuffs and collars may not have the same cosseting feel as more expensive jackets, but a budget cycling jacket remains the best option for cold-weather cycling as it'll still regulate body temperatures better than a raincoat, will flap around a lot less and can carry more food and essentials in its back pockets.

Jackets can have a hard life, as they're often worn for long winter rides in inclement weather, bombarded from above and below by rain and muck off the road. Regular washing and use wears them out and many cyclists have more than one to rotate according to weather conditions.

↓ Even a budget jacket will see plenty of use through the winter.

## Gilets

Not a jacket, nor a jersey, a gilet is a cycling waistcoat which can be very useful as a standby extra layer carried in the back pocket or as an all-day body warmer in cooler conditions. Materials vary but gilets are usually light in weight, with a wind or waterproof chest with a high collar, and often with mesh or lighter-weight material on the back. A full zip makes a gilet easy to get on and off even when riding along no-handed. To keep the weight down and help with stowage there won't normally be pockets on a gilet, although some may have a small one for a phone or essentials. A shower or waterproof gilet is a good option in spring and summer when it's worth keeping the body dry, less so the arms.

→ A gilet can be rolled up and carried in a back pocket in case of a shower or drop in temperature.

# Cycling tights

Full-length cycling tights should be worn in cold weather for most riding apart from racing. Cycling tights are an essential item in the cyclist's wardrobe and can cost as much as a premium cycling jacket. Most are of the bib type with the same thermal material or mesh panel extending up the lower back to shoulder straps that hold the tights up. The lower stomach may be secured with a zip, especially if it comes up as high as the ribs.

Traditional bib tights require the rider to wear a pair of cycling shorts underneath, but many tights these days are designed to be worn without shorts and are fitted with a conventional padded insert. Tights with an insert can be more comfortable and better fitting than shorts worn under unpadded tights, but it does mean they have to be washed a lot more often, whereas unpadded tights can be worn many times before going into the wash. Rotating shorts through the wash means you will never have to wait for your tights to dry before the next ride.

The legs of cycling tights should be tailored for a snug fit that doesn't

→ Full-length tights will get plenty of use throughout the year.

→ There's no need to wear shorts if the tights are fitted with a padded insert.

restrict pedalling and at the foot end there'll be a zipped closure or stirrups. A tailored pair will hang with a pronounced bend in them to account for the fact that the leg is never completely straight when pedalling.

Materials vary from the popular stretchy Roubaix type, which has a smooth windproof surface and soft lining, to thicker wind- and rain-resistant thermal materials intended for harsher conditions. The lighter thermal versions will suffice in all but the coldest temperatures but all-seasons riders may keep a pair of extra-warm and even rainproof tights for extreme cold and inclement cycling.

## Bib knicks

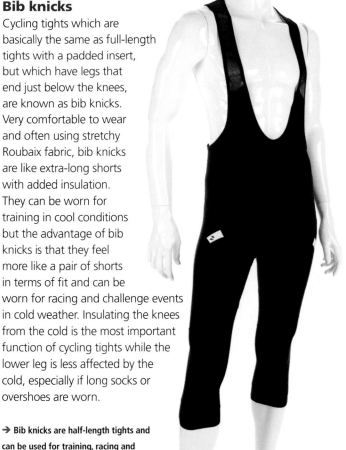

Cycling tights which are basically the same as full-length tights with a padded insert, but which have legs that end just below the knees, are known as bib knicks. Very comfortable to wear and often using stretchy Roubaix fabric, bib knicks are like extra-long shorts with added insulation. They can be worn for training in cool conditions but the advantage of bib knicks is that they feel more like a pair of shorts in terms of fit and can be worn for racing and challenge events in cold weather. Insulating the knees from the cold is the most important function of cycling tights while the lower leg is less affected by the cold, especially if long socks or overshoes are worn.

→ Bib knicks are half-length tights and can be used for training, racing and challenge events in cold weather.

# Leg and arm warmers

Cycling tights and long-sleeved tops are the preferred options for winter cycling in all but the coldest conditions but it's also possible to ride through much of the year wearing leg and arm warmers. These affordable and unassuming tubes of material are deceptively useful accessories that have the added benefit of rolling up small enough to be carried in the back pocket of a cycling top.

Materials vary, but like tights the most popular types use Roubaix fabric, which is warm and stretchy enough to cling to the arms and legs. They may have rubberised grippers at both ends but both leg and arm warmers rely on the elasticated hems on shorts and sleeves to prevent them slipping down.

Leg warmers can be full length, extending to the ankle, or they may end anywhere from below the knee to the ankle. They should be long enough to sit under the legs of the shorts at the top of the thigh, several inches above the hem of the shorts to ensure they don't slip down. Another plus for leg warmers is that they don't interfere with how the shorts sit and feel on the saddle, unlike tights, which can feel bunched up around the crotch area.

Arm warmers can only be used with short-sleeved jerseys and for that reason are less effective in wintry weather. Static arms feel the cold more than pedalling legs and most short-sleeved jerseys are made from thinner material designed for summer use. In winter it's better to wear thermal long-sleeved tops and jackets. Arm warmers are best suited to chilly spring rides and summer mornings and evenings. They can be pulled on in seconds and then whipped off and stowed in a back pocket as soon as the sun comes up.

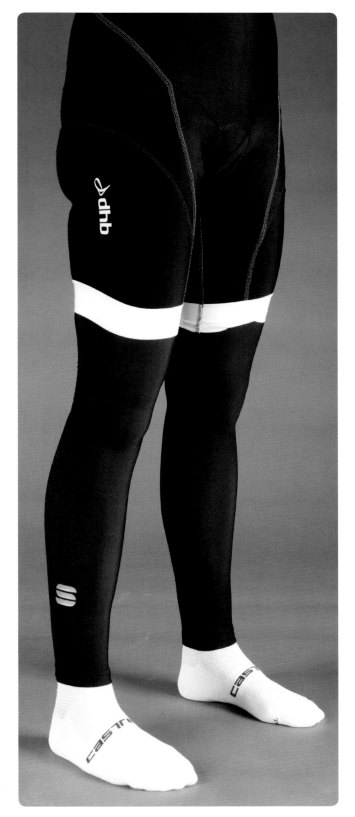

Plain Lycra arm warmers can be folded to little more than handkerchief dimensions; thermal arms are a little bulkier but easily stuffed into one back pocket. Check that the sleeves of the short-sleeved jersey have tight enough grippers to prevent the arm warmers slipping down, as it can be frustrating when they do. Having said that, there's about a 1° window when it can be quite pleasant to ride along with the breeze cooling two inches of exposed bicep.

**↑ → If you don't have full-length tights, knee or leg warmers are an affordable and effective alternative.**

# Extreme wet and cold weather gear

Many items of cycling clothing will insulate the rider and shrug off a shower of rain. Biking gear is, after all, outdoor clothing that's designed to be hard-wearing and versatile across a broad range of weather conditions. But there are times when those parameters are exceeded and if the temperature drops below about 5°C, or the rain is hammering down all day, then a few well-chosen extreme weather items can make the difference between an enjoyable ride and one that could land you with hypothermia.

## Soft shell and waterproof coats

Every cyclist gets caught out in heavy rain from time to time. A soft shell jacket with a waterproofing treatment can be rolled up and stashed in the back pocket of a jacket or jersey and is worth carrying whenever there's a chance of persistent rain. Quality versions using breathable materials can be worn in a variety of cold and damp conditions, and many cyclists happily wear their soft shell jackets for long rides. Racing versions of soft shell tops are tighter fitting and come with additional features like watertight neoprene cuffs. If you're serious about training in all weathers, it's worth trying one of these more expensive versions, but make sure it fits over your wet-weather base layer, jersey or jacket.

A budget waterproof cycling coat or cape or even a walker's cagoule is better than nothing if you get caught out in the rain. They can be hot and sweaty inside and some rain will probably

↑ A tight-fitting and breathable soft shell can keep heavy rain at bay for hours on end.

come through the seams, but anything is better than getting wet through when you're far from home. Wind chill on the bike will go right through wet clothing and is to be avoided at all costs.

↓ Anything is better than getting soaked to the skin.

## Thermal waterproof tops

Castelli's Gabba jacket pioneered the concept of a training and racing top with thermal and rain-repelling properties and

→ Castelli's Gabba top has achieved cult status for its performance in cold and wet races.

there's now a niche category for this type of high-tech jacket. Combining Gore-Tex Windstopper fabric with stretchy thermal materials, tops like the Gabba are tailored for a tight fit making them suited to racing in extreme weather conditions and for serious training rides. The material is water-repellent and won't prevent the top getting damp, but such is the close-fitting nature of these tops that they have something of a wetsuit effect. Pricey but well worth considering for racing, hard training and challenge rides in grotty weather.

## Neoprene gloves

If it's raining heavily a pair of neoprene gloves can help the hands to stay dry and warm. They should be tight-fitting with adjustable cuffs to prevent water draining inside the glove. Gloves with waterproof, breathable membranes can also work well in heavy rain, but the good thing about neoprene is that it holds its shape better than a glove made with lighter fabrics.

↑ Neoprene is ideal for gloves if riding for long periods during heavy rain.

## Lobster-claw gloves

For extreme cold weather riding there are gloves with a thumb and two wide fingers into which two fingers go on each side.

→ In very cold weather lobster-claw style gloves keep the fingers together for extra warmth.

These lobster-claw gloves radiate less heat than five-finger versions and mean that a thinner glove can be used on really cold days. However, they feel strange to wear at first and they aren't as dextrous as conventional gloves.

## Skull caps and headbands

The only way to keep the head warm under a helmet in cold weather is to wear a tight-fitting thermal or wicking skullcap or headband under the helmet. A well-vented cycling helmet feels like it's sucking air into and around the head and in winter it can feel seriously chilly. A thin skullcap or even a headband makes all the difference, but make sure your helmet has enough adjustment to fit securely over the extra material. For winter cycling it's worth buying a less vented helmet as it'll reduce cold draughts and keep the rain out too. Or you can tape over your regular summer helmet.

↓ In winter a thin headband or skullcap worn under the helmet keeps the head warm.

# Eyewear

→ **Eye protection is an important consideration at all times of year.**

Eye protection is a serious matter which every road cyclist should address, whatever the type or duration of their cycling. The primary function of eyewear for cycling is to cut down on bright sunlight with tinted lenses, but to that should be added protection from airborne particles and insects; enhancing vision in various light conditions; blocking damaging UV light from the eyes; and shielding the eyes from the wind.

Sports sunglasses can be worn on the bike but it's best to choose shades designed for cycling as they'll be designed to fit under a cycling helmet, with the arms outside the straps and lenses curved to aid lateral vision and cut down on draughts. Nose pieces and contact points should be made from materials that don't become uncomfortable when the rider is sweating.

Premium models are also likely to be very light and feature quality lenses with UV protection and vision-enhancing clarity, especially at the curved sides. Clear lenses with a Polaroid treatment can aid vision in low light and wet weather, as well as protecting the eyes from gritty water thrown up from the tyres. Anyone who's ridden behind a bike rider without mudguards will know just how much water is sprayed from the back wheel directly into the face of the rider behind.

Prices for cycling glasses are affected more by fashion and style than any other item of cycling kit. It isn't necessary to spend hundreds on the latest pair as worn by the winner of the Tour de France as there are many very effective and attractive alternatives at more affordable price points.

## Prescription cycling glasses

**Short-sighted spectacle-wearing cyclists are ill served when it comes to cycling shades. High street prescription sunglasses with lightweight plastic lenses can be worn but they won't be designed to fit securely on the nose or under a cycling helmet. Some brands of cycling glasses, however, offer a prescription lens option which can either be incorporated into the lens itself or made-up as a separate clear lens designed to sit inside the curved lens of the shades. Not all curved lenses will take a prescription for severely short-sighted riders so it's always worth checking with an optician what your options are.**

# Accessories

Some are more essential than others, but there's no end of extra things you can buy to add to your bike or to enhance your experience of cycling

## Computers

It doesn't seem like that long ago that the only battery-powered device to be found on a bicycle was a basic odometer displaying speed (max and average) and distance. Early bike computers employed a sensor attached to a spoke with a pick-up unit cable tied to the fork and a wire routed up the fork to the bars, where the computer was attached to a plastic bracket.

Wireless transmission has replaced wires but the component parts remain the same, with a wheel-mounted sensor and pick-

↑ Trek bikes incorporate a computer sensor into the offside chainstay.

↑ The Strava app on a smartphone records essential performance and route data.

up unit transmitting information to a bar-mounted computer. Calculations are based on wheel size including the tyre, which must to be programmed into the computer before use. Some are neater than others, with bike brands like Trek incorporating a sensor in their bicycle chainstays that picks up off the back wheel and can also display cadence from a sensor attached to the crank.

A basic computer costs little and is a useful tool, even if it's only used to show speed and distance covered. Premium versions use wireless transmission, better quality materials and longer-lasting batteries. Additional functions like cadence and heart rate, transmitted from a chest band, can be essential aids for specific training sessions.

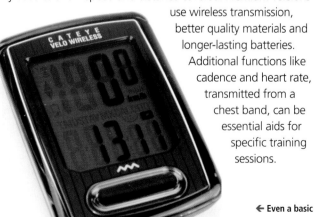

← Even a basic computer is useful for displaying speed and distance.

## GPS and smartphones

Recording rides remotely using a GPS function in either a cycling-specific computer or a smartphone has become at least as popular as conventional bike-mounted cycling computers. GPS tracks the rider's progress recording speed and distance; it also shows location and can be used to navigate around a pre-programmed route. Other features include the gear selected and estimates of heart rate, functional threshold power (FTP), VO2 max (see page 135).

After the ride, the unit or smartphone can connect to a computer and data from the ride downloaded. Much more detailed information is recorded from a GPS file, including climbing in metres for individual climbs plus total climbing metres, as well as segment splits and gradients, and if the appropriate sensors are fitted some will also record cadence and power.

Smartphones can also run apps such as Strava that not only record details of your ride but can also compare the data to other Strava users along recorded segments. In popular cycling regions there are few roads that haven't been carved up into Strava segments, and for many cyclists trying to better their times along favoured climbs or flat sections this has spiced up many a training ride. Strava doesn't show real-time information on the screen, however, so it can only be referenced after a ride.

## Power measuring

Measuring power output has taken over from heart rate as the most effective way to monitor effort levels in training and racing. Professional riders on road and track have been using chainset-mounted strain gauges since the 1980s, when the German SRM power crank was invented. Power was measurable before but only on a static, often lab-based ergometer, and the ability to get real-time power readouts on an SRM-equipped machine revolutionised coaching methods and in-race strategies.

The high cost of SRM-equipped cranks (the gauges are retro-fitted to the big brand component makers' chainsets) made them unaffordable to many hobby cyclists, but more affordable variants have recently come on to the market, like the PowerTap rear hub, Stages and Limits pedal-mounted system and the lightweight 4iiii crank sensor. These are connected either via wires or wirelessly to a head unit displaying power in Watts.

→ SRM produced the first mass-market power measuring system.

## Bottle cages

Maintaining hydration on even the shortest rides is essential and the time-honoured method is to carry a plastic bottle in a holder or cage attached to the down-tube, and often the seat-tube as well, of the frame. Bottle cages are made from plastic, steel, alloy and carbon, with aluminium the most popular as it combines extreme lightness with an affordable price. Plastic and steel cages are less favoured but carbon fibre has become popular as the lightest material that also matches the frames of many keen road cyclists' bikes.

Apart from one or two attempts to introduce new sizes and shapes of cycling bottle, or *bidon* as it's known in French, the industry standard is almost universally accepted (holding a minimum 500ml) and virtually all cages will accept standard diameter bottles.

Aluminium cages are springy enough to hold the bottle tightly in place and can be bent very gently for an even tighter fit, to prevent the bottle bouncing out over rough roads and cobbles.

→ Bottle cages are fixed to the frame with two hex bolts.

Carbon cages rely on a precise fit with a small amount of flex in them to allow the bottle to be inserted and extracted while on the move.

Cages may look different to each other but they all do the same job, and while it's possible to spend extra on the lightest carbon versions, often the most traditional-looking models using thin aluminium tubes work the best and can be matched to the bike, as they often come in a variety of anodised finishes.

## Cycling bottle essentials

Cycling bottles come in a standard diameter but they can vary in capacity from 500ml to 750ml, with the bigger sizes extending well beyond the bottle cage. When full it's even more important to ensure that the cage has sufficient tension in it to hold the bottle securely on bumpy roads. It should also be noted that two full 750ml bottles will add 1.5kg to the weight of the bike.

There are also numerous nozzle types, from the basic hard plastic pull-up valve to bite-and-suck types similar to ones found on backpack hydration bladders. Bladder-type hydration packs are unnecessary for most road rides, as they hold too much fluid, weigh heavily on the back and can be hot and uncomfortable in summer. For trekking rides in the heat where water is scarce a bladder may be convenient or even essential.

For rides over three hours it's best to take two bottles, stopping briefly to fill them if needed. Most challenge rides have fuel stops, which allow many riders to get by on one bottle, and in a race the best option is to throw the used bottle to a helper who then hands up a filled replacement.

Many bottles are made with biodegradable plastics that last a long time but are more easily damaged if dropped. It's very important to clean bottles regularly, especially if energy drinks are used, as bacteria can form in the base and around the inside of the cap. Inspect bottles for telltale black marks in the base and wash the bottle and cap in a dishwasher if possible.

Thermally insulated bottles that keep liquids either hot or extra

## Pro bottles

Professional cyclists use dozens of quality bottles every time they race, and if you can't beg one from a rider at the finish of a race the best way to get one is in the race feed zones and up to about one kilometre beyond it, where the riders jettison their bottles and replace them with fresh ones from their feed bags. You may also pick up a brightly coloured team feed bag or 'musette' as well as a free gel or energy bar, but watch out for race vehicles and other sharp-elbowed Wombles!

↑ A pro bike race is a useful place to pick up a free bottle.

cold are worth considering for extreme conditions, and flat aero bottles that require a special cage are also found on some aero time trial machines.

## Pumps and tyre inflators

Every cyclist needs at least two types of pump: one for pumping up the tyres at home and another for putting air into them when out on the road. At home a stirrup, floor or track pump is by far the most effective and easy way to pump tyres to high pressures. Gripping the handles of the pump and bending your knees to move the piston vertically up and down the barrel is by far the best and easiest way to put more than 100psi into a tyre. Trying to achieve those pressures with a traditional hand-pump is, as every cyclist knows only too well, torture on the biceps.

On the road a more portable solution is required, and was traditionally served by a long plastic or metal hand-pump clipped along the underside of the top tube or in front of the seat tube. These frame-fitting pumps had a nozzle that connected directly to the valve and with some determined pumping could get close to recommended pressures.

Long frame-fitting pumps can be inserted into steel or aluminium frames but they aren't suited to carbon frames with bottom bracket and top tube junctions, which are too wide and smoothly arched to hold the pump under tension. Mini-pumps are the solution – they don't have the pumping power of a longer pump but they can be carried in a back pocket or clipped to a bracket alongside the bottle cage. Mini-pumps will put air into the tyre, but achieving high pressures takes a great many frustratingly short thrusts.

Designs have improved and it's also worth paying more for

→ A floor-mounted track or stirrup pump is the only way to achieve high pressures at home.

← A mini-pump is the most popular inflator, carried in the back pocket or on a frame-mounted clip.

a premium model that may not be the shortest but has a metal barrel with a fold-out T-handle. Pumps last for many years, and your home pump and ride pump will become trusted companions and friends; choose them wisely and get the best you can afford. There's another solution to the mid-ride puncture. Gas canister inflators with cycling-specific nozzles are the most compact solution of all and can inflate a tyre to high pressures in a few seconds. The amount of air going into the tyre can be controlled, allowing the canister to be used more than once. For riders with tubeless tyres a gas canister is the best way to build pressure fast enough to seat the bead on the rim in the event of a tyre change.

→ Gas inflators.

↑ Many cyclists use a flashing rear light in daylight hours.

## Rear lights

A set of bike lights should be in every cyclist's essentials box, even if night riding isn't on the agenda. Many riders choose not to cycle at night but there are numerous days throughout the year when a ride overruns into dusk or even night, or more often when low light conditions render visibility less than 20/20. Add to that unusual conditions like mist and fog and it makes sense for every rider to have, at the very least, a small rear light to hand.

The safety imperative in these circumstances is to make the cyclist's presence known to vehicles approaching from behind. A red rear light is the most effective way to pierce the gloom and the modern LED type can be seen from several hundred metres away. A rear light at dusk or night could save your life.

A simple LED rear light is inexpensive, light in weight and easy to attach to the seatpost of a bike using the preferred option of a thick rubber band. Powered by battery or rechargeable cell (often by USB), a back light can last for a few hours before recharging.

More expensive rear lights have longer-lasting batteries, better build quality using lightweight materials and all the modes you'll ever need. Functions on all rear lights are likely to range from flashing options to continuous, with the flashing setting giving the longest run time. Some will also have an intense daylight mode that's surprisingly effective on everything but the sunniest days.

Rear lights are especially popular with British time triallists who use them on their low-profile aero bikes during early morning and evening events when the light quality is poor and motorists aren't expecting to see cyclists on busier roads used for set-distance events.

Using a rear light during the day is a personal safety decision that many riders opt to pass up on. It's worth carrying a small emergency rear light on those occasions when the ride might overrun into the dusk or if you're on a long A to B ride, such

↓ It's worth carrying a rear light as an emergency backup, especially on an all-day ride.

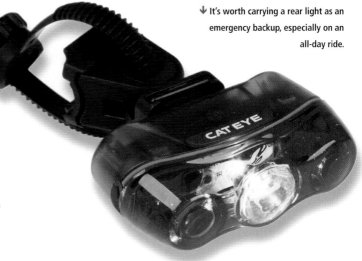

## Lights and the law

**The legal requirement regarding bicycle lights in the UK is to have a white light on the front, red at the rear and reflectors on the rear and pedals. It's very unlikely you'll be stopped if you don't have the reflectors, but you will if you don't have the lights! A flashing red rear light is also permissible.**

as on a touring holiday, when it's quite easy to underestimate the distance and time taken. Fatigue or unscheduled stops for punctures, for instance, can easily lengthen the day into early evening or night. If the intention is to ride into or at night, it can also be wise to carry *two* rear lights, either for extra visibility or to have one light in reserve in case the active light runs out of charge.

### Front lights

A front light is essential in towns at night as the danger from vehicles pulling out from side streets or across junctions is far greater than on country roads. Everything that can be done to make the rider visible from the front should be done to ensure motorists, who are often making hurried short journeys, can see an approaching rider.

The other function of the front light is to illuminate the road ahead, allowing the rider to see where he or she is going and picking out potentially dangerous bumps and potholes. Any type of country road cycling demands that riders use a powerful front light, as there's nothing more terrifying then bombing down a descent when you can't quite see the bends, potholes and gravel patches.

Front lights use more powerful halogen bulbs than the LED type used in rear lights and the batteries are bigger to satisfy the extra draw on power.

Rechargeable batteries can vary from standard sizes to the biggest types, which fit inside the bottle cage or hang from the top tube and connect to the light unit via cables.

The most powerful front lights are bright enough to completely illuminate the road and dazzle oncoming traffic. Build quality is high with prices to match, and these premium fronts are popular with riders who regularly ride at night. Mid-price options clip into handlebar-mounted brackets or use a rubber-

↑ A powerful front light is essential for night-time riding on unlit country roads.

band mounting system. The battery is housed internally and functions include continuous at high and low intensities as well as flashing modes. Budget front lights shouldn't be relied on for extended night-time rides but can be useful as a get-you-home and when it may be more important to be seen than to illuminate the way.

↓ Powerful front lights can be expensive, but for serious night riding they're worth saving for.

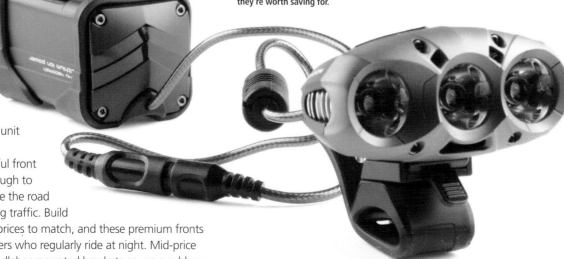

↑ **High-vis clothing and accessories can be effective in low light conditions.**

## Hi-vis clothing and accessories

Many items of cycling clothing have reflective details or piping that can be very effective at night when illuminated by vehicle lights. High visibility clothing serves a different function in that it works better in low light conditions and doesn't require an external light source to catch the eye.

Yellow and orange hi-vis soft shell tops and jackets are popular among road cyclists, many of whom will happily wear a loose fitting hi-vis raincoat for long rides, putting safety ahead of comfort and wind drag. Hi-vis tops are available in quality breathable fabrics but many aren't made of such materials, and if being seen is a priority it may be worth investing in a rear light with a daylight mode and stowing the raincoat in the back pocket for when it rains.

Hi-vis makes a lot of sense for urban cyclists, where a bright colour can stand out against busy or dark backgrounds, alerting vehicles and pedestrians to your presence. Hi-vis backpack covers with reflective details are affordable and very effective for commuter cyclists to be seen, and even smaller items like gloves and overshoes can be surprisingly eye-catching.

## Saddle packs and luggage

Only a few items can be carried in the rear pockets of a cycling jersey or jacket, but backpacks are uncomfortable and hot for cycling in. The best way to carry additional items is to put them into a saddle pack or a bike-mounted luggage system.

Saddle packs are pouches that sit directly under the saddle and come in various sizes, the smallest holding little more than an inner tube and three tyre levers. Road cyclists have always carried spare tubes and tyres on their bikes and before saddle packs they were wrapped in a piece of thick plastic or cloth and secured under the saddle with a leather or nylon toe strap threaded through the saddle rails. Alternatively a plastic water bottle with the top cut off served as a tube and tyre holder, ideally in a cage on the seat tube with the down tube cage carrying a standard bottle.

A saddle pack is well worth fitting to every road bike and should only be taken off if the bike is being used for a race. They're light, compact and easy to either clip on to a bracket under the saddle or secure with Velcro straps. Inner tubes and tyre levers are ideal items to put in, but bigger packs can also be used to carry a multi-tool and maybe a mini pump or gas canister and emergency rear light. Be sure to wrap tubes and lights to protect them from rubbing inside the pack. Stowing essentials in a seat pack takes the stress out of finding scattered items before every ride and means all you may need in your back pockets are a phone, a rain jacket and some emergency cash.

For overnight rides and touring it's best to fit a rack on to which various sized packs and panniers can be attached. Check that the bike has the correct threaded mounting points near the top of the seat stays and above the rear dropouts, as without them it won't be possible to fit a rack without using ugly additional brackets. A bike with these mounting points should also have been engineered to handle the extra payload of rack and luggage. Panniers vary from small weekender or commuter types to bigger volume bags suitable for cycling holidays and trips of a week or more.

➔ **A small saddle pack will take an inner tube and tyre levers.**

➔ **Panniers are attached to a rack mounted to the back end of the bike.**

# Transporting and storing

Bikes aren't big or heavy machines but as soon as you want to transport them or even store them at home they become frustratingly unwieldy trip hazards. And don't even ask about tandems! A bicycle has bars and pedals that stick out and flick round just when you don't want them to. Even just putting one into a shed can be tricky, as pedals and bars can easily catch on other items.

Whatever the dwelling or storage facility there's a number of wall-mounted racks and hooks that can hang multiple bikes out of harm's way. Small secure specialist bike storage units are also worth looking at, as keeping a bike in the garden shed is asking for a spade to be dropped on to it.

Carrying bikes in cars is another chore as only the biggest estate cars and people carriers can swallow a bike with both wheels in place. To get a bike into a hatchback requires the removal of at least the front wheel, and involves folding the rear seats flat. Care must also be taken not to scratch or damage the interior of the car, and the bike needs to be carefully laid down with the front wheel stowed where it can't rub on the frame.

For many cyclists the only option is to carry bikes on a boot or roof-mounted rack. Many versions and variants of car bike racks are available at all price points; it's just a case of deciding your budget and whether you prefer to have a removable boot rack or more permanent roof rack.

Carrying a bike externally on a vehicle makes it more vulnerable to wet weather, thieves and damage. There's not a lot that can be done if you have a long drive in the rain with bikes on the roof, but oiling the chain, drying out the bar tape and seat and checking the main bearings in the headset, hubs and bottom bracket should all be essential maintenance jobs if bikes are regularly transported this way. Locking the bikes to the rack

↑ There are many storage options for bikes in houses and sheds.

is also worth doing, even if it's a relatively ineffective deterrent to opportunists. Many modern racks incorporate a locking mechanism in the frame or wheel clamp.

Finally, bikes on roofs and the back of smaller cars will add much to the height of the car or could stick out at the sides. The risk is that the bike can hit height or width restriction bars and low tunnels, with very damaging consequences for both bike and the vehicle itself. Put a sticker on the steering wheel with 'Bikes!' on it, as a reminder to yourself when you're driving.

↓ A removable boot-mounted rack is a popular way to carry bikes on the back of a car.

↓ The best way to carry multiple bikes on a car is on a roof-mounted rack.

# Ride tools

Even the most maintenance-averse rider should have a multi-tool that can be carried in the back pocket or saddle pack. At the very least a multi-tool with hex keys in 4, 5 and 6mm sizes can be used to adjust bars, stems, headsets, seatposts, saddles and shoeplates, which can come loose or require adjustment mid-ride. Hex keys are also required for checking bottle cage mounts, brake blocks and mudguards.

A multi-tool should also have flat and cross-headed bits that can be used to fine-tune front and rear derailleur settings. Many include a chain splitter, which, even if only ever used once, could make the difference between getting home and being stranded with a broken chain. Some multi-tools incorporate pliers, tyre levers and a spoke key but it's worth weighing up – literally – the likelihood of needing these extra tool against their additional bulk and weight.

↑ A multi-tool will have a variety of bike-specific bits to adjust and repair minor issues on your bike.

## 'No-tools' cycling

Such is the build quality of most modern machines that it's quite possible to ride through the seasons without ever needing more than a couple of tyre levers and a spare tube. It's unusual for the parts of a well put-together machine to give any trouble after some initial checks and adjustments.

For many riders the decision to ride with no more than a spare tube, levers and pump is one that's worth the risk. In the event of a mechanical failure or serious issue a resourceful cyclist can often borrow a tool from a house or workshop, or another passing cyclist. If all else fails a phone call will summon your other half (for a big favour in return!) or a cab to recover chastened rider and machine. Consequently always carry a mobile phone when cycling.

When a bike is new or has had a rebuild it makes sense to carry at least a couple of hex keys to make adjustments to seat height, saddle position and the angle of the bars during the ride. Riding's the best way to tinker with your position – sitting on the bike in the kitchen isn't the same.

→ The only fiddling you are likely to do on a modern bike is with the settings on your bike computer.

# Turbo trainers

Indoor training on a bike attached to a static trainer or turbo has taken off in recent times and the great number and variety of indoor trainers is proof of the demand for a wide range of indoor training options. From the most basic fold-up turbo with an open fan to the most sophisticated integrated indoor trainers, it's possible to create an indoor training environment to achieve high levels of fitness.

A simple turbo trainer consists of a strong floor-mounted base usually with fold-out legs to which a roller and resistance unit are attached. The back end of the bike is locked into place using a lever-actuated cam situated on the arms of the turbo above the roller. This locks on to the ends of the quick-release lever and barrel adjuster in the back wheel. It's worth using an old skewer for this, as it'll get scratched by the slotted clamps. Once the back wheel is secured the roller can be adjusted on to the back

tyre so that it rests gently on the tyre without slipping under acceleration. Once locked in place the bike is held very securely and won't fall over however hard the rider pedals. Resistance levels are altered through the gears, giving a wide range of pedalling speeds and resistances.

If the rider intends to do regular sessions on the turbo it's worth using a turbo-specific rear tyre designed to absorb heat generated from friction on the roller, which can damage the carcass of a light road tyre and wear out the tread. A slick turbo tyre should also run more quietly on the roller. To prevent wear and tear on expensive rear wheels it can also be worth buying a sturdy yet budget rear wheel, fitted with a new cassette and turbo-specific tyre. This wheel can be swapped in and out of the bike for indoor training.

When the machine is installed in the turbo the back end is

← A basic turbo trainer has fold-out legs and can be used with a standard road bike.

→ More sophisticated turbo trainers can be programmed for a variety of training sessions.

lifted off the ground a few inches and many riders like to chock the front wheel with a plastic wheel dish or something like a block of wood. One more item is essential when riding the turbo – a towel to drape over the bars and top tube to catch corrosive sweat dripping into the headset bearing and on to the top tube. It's useful for mopping the face too.

More expensive turbo trainers use the same mounting system as a basic turbo and at the very least should have a resistance unit that runs more smoothly and quietly than the most basic fan versions. Additional features usually include sensors in the turbo which link to a readout on the bars or on a screen supplied with the turbo showing speed, distance, power, time elapsed and so on. Training programmes loaded into the software can take the guesswork out of a session too. You can even compete in a virtual race on screen that can make indoor training significantly more entertaining and rewarding.

For the most dedicated indoor training enthusiast there are machines like the Wattbike that don't need a 'donor' bike and are more like the spinning machines seen in gyms. A cycling trainer of this type accurately measures and displays the power output of the rider and can be used to follow a power-based programme from a coach. The position is fully adjustable and can be fine-tuned with the rider's preferred saddle and pedals. Wattbikes are used by most cycling federations and professional teams to assess rider potential and levels of fitness.

← ↓ Indoor trainers like the Wattbike allow the rider to follow routines based on power output.

# Old school indoor training

Rollers are very different to turbo trainers in that the rider isn't supported and there's no resistance in the rollers themselves. Rollers are simple devices which feature twin sets of rollers or drums attached to a steel frame, with the front rollers linked to the rears with a rubber driving band. A bike is placed on to the drums with the front and rear wheels resting on both sets of rollers. The rider carefully mounts the machine (a handhold is useful) and, balancing, begins to pedal gently as both front and rear wheels spin around. Gyroscopic forces keep the bike upright and once up to speed the cyclist can change gear and ride at every cadence.

Rollers are marvellous things but rarely used for indoor training as they're not as easy or effective as a turbo. But they're great for honing pedalling style and warming up and down and remain popular with track riders. Competition rollers link two sets of rollers to a board with two big pointers, one for each rider, who must pedal as fast they can to bring their pointer around the 'clock' before the other rider. Cadences of around 170rpm can be reached with a helper holding the machine as the rider gives it everything.

→ Rollers are great for honing pedalling style and speed.

# Virtual-ride packages

Programs and apps like Zwift offer interactive indoor training that places the rider on some of the most famous cycling roads and mountains in the world. Displayed on a laptop or computer screen is the actual image of the road, with progress shown according to the effort being made by the rider. These programs can even put them into a virtual bunch of riders in a race scenario. Other riders on the same program can race each other in real time in the latest versions and there's even talk of putting a virtual rider into actual footage from a professional race. A conventional turbo can be used but the bike ideally needs to have an ANT+ sensor relaying speed and cadence to the head unit. Ideally a power meter will also transmit power outputs too.

→ With a virtual racing package it's possible to compete with riders from anywhere in the world.

# CHAPTER 5
# BIKE SET-UP

**Saddle, handlebars and pedals are the contact points between rider and machine and their shape and orientation play a big part in bike set-up. This chapter will help you find the base settings for a comfortable and efficient riding position.**

When you see a professional racing cyclist in action, it often looks as if they've become one with their bike. Moving their hands from the top to the lower part of the handlebars, accessing the brakes, rising out of the saddle to pedal 'standing up' – all this looks harmonious and natural. The smoothly turning legs, the stationary position of the pelvis, the arms at a slight angle, enabling fast reactions at all times – rider and bike are in perfect harmony.

This intimate connection between rider and bike is the result of clocking up thousands of miles per year. Another reason is that racing cyclists adjust and check their position on the bike extremely meticulously, and this, but not necessarily their actual upper-body riding position, is one of the habits of professional cyclists that it pays a keen road rider to adopt too.

Considering how differently individual humans are made it's hardly surprising that bike fitting is an approximate science, using a mixture of theory and 'feel'. However, there are a some tried and tested guidelines to adhere to.

# Seat height and angle

Finding the correct seat height will maximise your pedalling style and power. The leg shouldn't be over-extended at the bottom of the pedal stroke because that can cause the pelvis to tilt or rock from side-to-side when the pedals reach the lowest point of the pedal circle. Nor should the knee be too bent, as that will reduce leg power and push the knee into the chest.

You can roughly find your correct saddle height by sitting on the saddle and putting the heel of your foot (in cycling shoes) on the pedal – which should be at the lowest point of its circle. Your leg should be almost fully straightened. Ideally, the shoe cleat should then engage with the pedal with the knee at a slight angle. Remember that it's better to have the saddle a little too low rather than too high – this method will ensure that the saddle's at the lower end of your base setting.

As a general rule a slightly lower seat height lowers the centre of gravity and aids a faster pedalling style on shorter to average

cranks (165–172.5mm). The pedalling circle also reduces the distance the knee travels towards the chest on each revolution.

A seat set at the top of your base setting, when the leg is almost straight at the bottom of the circle, can suit riders who prefer to push bigger gears at lower cadences. It can also suit a long-legged rider on cranks of 175mm or longer. The more open angle of the knee allows the rider to get 'on top' of the gear. If knee pain is experienced when the knee is at more of an angle a higher saddle may alleviate this too.

### The LeMond and Burke methods

There are various formulas for determining saddle height. One of the most popular, devised by Tour de France champion Greg LeMond, involves measuring from the top of the crotch to the floor in bare feet. That inseam figure is then multiplied by 0.883, which gives the saddle height taken from the centre of the bottom bracket to the top of the saddle.

Another trusted method was devised by respected coach Ed Burke. This sets the seat on the higher side of a base setting:

- Stand in cycling shoes and shorts with feet 5cm apart.
- Shove a book between your legs.
- Measure from floor to top edge of book.
- Multiply by 1.09.
- Set seat height with crank pointing down but in line with seat tube. Take it from pedal axle to top of centre of saddle.

## Different cleat stack heights

Remember that if you have more than one bike with different pedal systems, especially if one has MTB-type SPD pedals, there can be a few millimetres' difference in stack height between different shoe cleat types. Measuring seat height from the pedal axle to the top of the saddle also accounts for different crank lengths and seat profiles.

↑ Correct saddle height. There should be a slight bend in the knee when the foot is at the bottom of the pedal stroke.

↑ Saddle too high.

↑ Saddle should not be lower than this.

# Knee and hip angle

A professional bike fitter may use an angle-measuring tool called a goniometer to measure the angle of the knee or the hip when the leg is at the bottom of the pedal stroke. Knee angle should be between 25°–35°. The hip angle comes into play more when the rider is trying to adopt a very aero riding position, especially on a time trial bike.

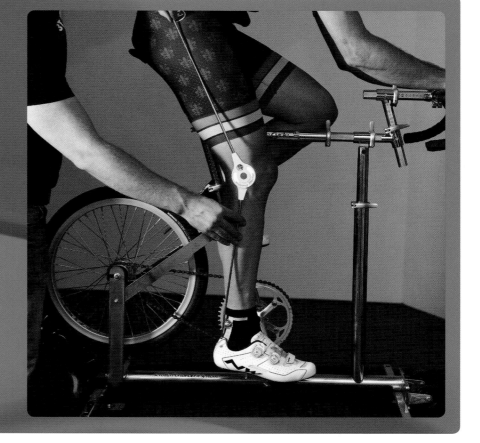

→ A very aero riding position can result in more acute hip angles.

## Low seat, high bars

Having the seat too low, the bars too high and not far enough away is a very common set-up mistake made by cyclists. Many riders assume this riding position will be more comfortable for their back as well as making it easier to put their feet down; but a low seat with high bars can actually cause back and knee pain. Raising the saddle and lowering the bars and adding a centimetre or two for reach shifts the weight forward and allows the legs to turn more freely. Bikes with tall head tubes are designed to offer a higher riding position at the front, so make sure the bars aren't stacked too high on the steerer.

➜ Seat too low/bars too high puts too much weight on your behind.

## Knee over the pedal

With the saddle set at the correct height ideally the knee should sit directly above the ball of your foot/pedal axle when the pedal arrives at the three o'clock position – horizontal and pointing forwards. With the pedal in this position and your foot in cycling shoes clipped in, hang a plumb line from the front of the knee.

The weighted end should hang within a centimetre of the pedal axle. Moving the saddle along its rails can fine-tune knee position above the axle and normally that should be enough. If the knee is a long way too far behind or in front of the pedal, however, the cranks or frame may be the wrong size.

## Saddle angle

For the base settings the saddle should always be set as flat and level as possible. Use a spirit level to get it spot on. Once you have the bike set up to your liking, if you're still not comfortable it can be worth tipping the nose of the saddle a very small amount either up or down. Time triallists sometimes favour a nose-down saddle that tips them slightly further forward of the pedals into a more aero position. Women may also find it more comfortable. A saddle with the nose slightly tipped up stops the rider slipping forward. If neither option works, it's best to try another type of saddle.

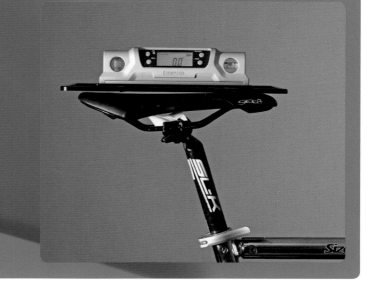

# Front end and torso

If you're a newcomer to road cycling, it's not advisable to copy the extreme aerodynamic riding positions adopted by many professional cyclists. The payback after your first ride could be pains in the neck, wrists and backside.

Your riding position should enable you to comfortably reach all handlebar positions including the upper handlebar (tops), the lower handlebar (drops) and the brake levers, for extended periods. If you find that you always leave your hands on the tops and ride with your elbows locked out, thereby transferring each bump on the road surface through to your neck and head, this is a clear indication that the handlebars are set too low and the stem (reach) is too long.

For new riders, it's tempting to set the stem slightly high. The top part of the saddle should, however, always be higher than where you'd rest your hands on the tops. Pro cyclists, though, may have their saddle set about 100mm higher than their handlebars. See Chapter 8 for advice on how to alter the height of your stem.

## On the drops

The best way to determine the correct distance between saddle and handlebar is to sit on the bike and place your hands on the drops. This position is the lowest from an aerodynamic point of view. Ideally your upper arm and forearm should be slightly bent, with the knees almost touching the elbows when pedalling. If your knees actually touch your elbows this means the stem is too short – unless you deliberately want to sit upright using the tops. When riding on the drops or on the brake hoods the arms should

### Bike fit at home

**Mount your bike on a turbo-trainer and position it in front of a large mirror. You can then make adjustments to your riding position comfortably, and under realistic conditions. However, pay attention to the position of your bike – it must be horizontal! You may have to place a chock under the front wheel to achieve this. Another good way to check your position is to get a friend to take photos or film you while you ride on the turbo.**

be bent at an angle not dissimilar to your leg at the bottom of the pedal stoke. Ideally your back should be reasonably straight and not too hunched or upright. It doesn't have to be horizontal to the ground or completely flat like a pro.

Handlebar shape, size and angle all play a big part in the front-end riding position, as does the position and shape of the brake levers. All these things are a matter for personal preference and over time you'll find the combination that suits you best. It's not just about your riding position either – the front end is the cockpit of the bike, from where the rider steers, changes gear and brakes, and it's crucial that everything falls confidently and easily to hand.

It can take quite a few goes to come up with exactly the right handlebar set-up but once you have it's well worth noting the components and their relative positions for future reference.

⬇ **Correct torso position.**

⬇ **Too hunched.**

⬇ **Too stretched out.**

# CHAPTER 6
# FITNESS AND TRAINING

The fitter you are the more you'll enjoy riding. On flat roads you can fly along with that satisfying feeling of power without pain. On climbs the legs spin around as you focus on holding your effort level just this side of the burn. Sprinting out of the saddle you get to enjoy the terrific sensation of the machine alive underneath you as the scenery begins to blur as you accelerate towards the horizon.

In addition to fitness it's essential to have the skills to control the machine at a range of speeds, which once mastered will make you a safer rider as well as a faster one. Bike-handling skills and the roadcraft of riding in a group of cyclists or in traffic are vital for your safety but they also greatly enrich the enjoyment of cycling as an exciting pastime. None of this is possible on a bike that doesn't fit properly, so that's another important thing to get right before you start riding your bike more seriously.

# General fitness

If you're starting to ride more seriously but have come from another sport, your general fitness and conditioning will have an effect on how quickly you adapt to riding a bike. Rugby and football players and swimmers, for instance, are likely to have excellent general fitness levels but could be carrying upper body muscle that isn't much use for cycling and would in effect be detrimental to power-to-weight ratios. The same goes for a rower, although they can compensate with additional leg power.

Runners also have high levels of aerobic ability, and tend to have lighter upper bodies and can often adapt very quickly to cycling, especially on hilly terrain. Runners lack the power of a trained cyclist, however, and will need to focus on that to build leg strength and power. Folk who train in gyms, on the other hand, especially if that includes spinning classes and weight training on the legs, can adapt to cycling very quickly and reach above-average levels in a matter of months.

So it's possible to come into cycling with good general levels of fitness and enjoy riding the bike for an hour or so at a steady and enjoyable pace. But if you want to go further and faster, you'll need to start riding your bike on a regular basis, preferably following even the most rudimentary of training plans.

### The five Ss of fitness
- **Stamina** – riding easily from one hour to all-day.
- **Speed** – using all-round fitness and technique to go faster.
- **Strength** – having the power to accelerate and sprint.
- **Skill** – using bike handling and pedalling technique to ride quickly and safely.
- **Spirit** – motivation and love of the sport to set goals and push through the tough times.

← Sportives have attracted many new cyclists from other sports.

## Dear diary

A desk or electronic diary is a useful tool for any cyclist with challenge rides or races to plan, but it's also a great way to monitor your fitness progress. Every ride should be logged, even if it's just time on the bike or distance covered. To that can be added as much information as you wish, including average speeds, heart rates and power outputs, although it's likely that if you're using a power meter or even a riding/training app then these stats will be automatically stored. But it's still hard to beat a visual representation, either on the page or on screen, showing how your training is progressing from week to week and month to month.

→ Track your progress digitally or on paper, it's the best way to work towards your goals.

### What kind of rider are you?

It's worth having a think about what kind of road cycling you want to do and what your goals are, short, medium and long-term. If you're starting from a relatively modest fitness, base you should give yourself six months before you pencil in your first significant event or challenge.

It's well worth getting a diary and putting some target dates into it, as this will enable you to isolate the training periods up to each one, with hard and easy blocks ensuring you get to each one in the best shape you can be. A target doesn't have to be a particular event, race or challenge ride; it could simply be to maintain a steady pace around your favourite circuit, or ride up a local climb in a certain time. Or it may be health or skills related – hitting a target weight, for instance, or riding comfortably in a group of riders over a set distance. Many goals are measurable or culminate in a single event, and making a commitment to work towards a target can be a strong motivational tool when the spirit is flagging.

It's not for everyone, though, and some riders may prefer to ride when it suits them purely for the enjoyment and general fitness benefits. It's possible to get very fit this way, although it can catch you out if you then decide to ride in a group event only to find that your level isn't the same as the more methodically trained entrants.

## Medical check-up

It's well worth getting checked over by a doctor if you're new to cycling or planning to increase your training load. If you're diabetic, the doctor can advise on diet or refer you to a nutritionist. Most important is to get the all-clear for any underlying heart issues that may require medication or further tests. A basic health check won't normally include an in-depth heart investigation, which can be expensive but a potential life-saver in the long-run.

# It's not just about the legs

Cycling is great for cardiovascular fitness and will give you strong legs but it doesn't build upper body strength and can lead to a weak core, back and arms. The good news is that a relatively small amount of time devoted to your upper body will benefit your cycling and help to balance upper and lower body strength.

Training to improve your endurance and power on the bike are central to meeting your cycling challenges, but there's a lot more to becoming a complete cyclist. Apart from improving your fitness these are the main elements that you should also consider:

- Adapting the body to the saddle, handlebars and riding position.
- Working on your pedalling style.
- Adapting to different cadences.
- General bike handling.
- More advanced bike handling in groups and downhill.

### THE PLANK

- ❏ Keep body as flat as possible with elbows at right angles directly under shoulders
- ❏ Three sets of 30 seconds, going up in 10 second blocks to one minute
- ❏ Good for core and stabilising muscles

### FLOOR BRIDGE

- ❏ Feet flat on floor a shoulder-width apart. Raise pelvis, squeezing glutes till body is in straight line

- ❏ Slowly lower pelvis just above the floor then raise again. Repeat eight to 12 times
- ❏ Good for glutes and stabilising muscles in lower back

### JACK-KNIFE

- ❏ Keep body straight with arms directly below shoulders. Make sure ankles are fully supported on ball
- ❏ Keeping the body straight, slowly draw the knees

towards your chest. Hold for a second and repeat eight to 12 times
- ❏ Good for hip flexor muscles, core and shoulder stability

## BACK EXTENSIONS

- ❑ With feet against a wall and a shoulder width apart, support pelvis on ball. Flexing your glutes and hamstring muscles, raise the upper body from the hip until the body is in a straight line
- ❑ Return slowly to the prone position and repeat six to 12 times
- ❑ Good for lower back strength

## BAR BELL LIFTS

- ❑ Support neck and shoulders on ball. Head back in neutral position with feet a shoulder width apart and supported by glutes
- ❑ Use core to maintain stability as you raise and lower bar bell in sets of 12
- ❑ Good for upper body strength, arms and core

## RUSSIAN TWISTS

- ❑ Keep back and shoulders straight, chin off chest and follow hands/bar bell with head during rotation
- ❑ With feet flat on floor and knees bent, lean back until abs tighten. Keeping hips square, slowly rotate with hands together or holding bar bell. Repeat on other side in sets of six to 12. Lift legs to make it harder
- ❑ Good for the sides of the core, promoting stability on the bike

## The principles of training

■ **Endurance**  ■ **Power/speed**  ■ **Technique**

If you want to ride a bike comfortably at a steady pace for anything more than a half-hour or so, you'll need to train your legs and body to achieve even this most basic goal. Road cycling is a multi-faceted pastime but it's primarily a sport that requires the same levels of discipline and training as any other athletic activity.

Few people would throw on a pair of running shoes and go bounding off on a ten-mile run without putting in at least a month or more in training, preferably with a steady build-up of short easy runs through to longer endurance efforts. Cycling is just the same and will more than reward the rider who follows even the most basic training programme tailored to a future target.

The principles of training need not be complicated, especially if the goal – probably the most popular one in cycling – is to cover from roughly 100km (60 miles) to 160km (100 miles) at a respectable average speed of above 25kph (15mph). It could be less, of course, or a lot more, but the basic foundation of your training will initially be to build up your endurance base.

Once the endurance phase is under way and a base level of fitness has been acquired, to endurance riding can be added drills or exercises to improve power and speed. These are very important, as they stress the muscles and their delivery systems and lead to encouraging improvements in average speeds as well as an improved ability to sprint and climb.

So endurance and power are the two most important elements of cycling fitness. Both can be achieved through riding, either on the road or on an indoor trainer. The third, often overlooked, element to work on is technique, which covers many things from pedalling style through to gear selection and bike handling. It's not enough to be a fit person on a bike, as you'll be left far behind if you can't select the correct gear, go smoothly around a corner or ride out of the saddle.

⬇ Good riding technique is another facet of 'training'.

## Make sure the bike fits

Before embarking on a training programme it's essential that your bike is the correct size and is set up to enable you to get the most out of your effort comfortably and without the risk of a strain or injury. The bike should also have a wide range of gears for all types of terrain and cadences.

Many bike shops offer a bike-fitting service for purchasers of new machines, but it's also possible to have your current riding position assessed and adjusted. An independent bike fitter will usually have a specialist rig that can be used to find your ideal riding position and the results can then be used for your 'base settings' every time you set up a bike. For more advice on setting up you bike see Chapter 5.

# Training off the bike

Most riders can benefit from weight training, especially on the legs. Muscle wastage in middle age, more than the decline in lung and heart function, affects cyclists more than other athletes. While it's possible to do muscle-building power drills on the bike it's more effective to follow a weight-training programme tailored for cycling.

And all cyclists should work on strengthening their core muscles, which help stabilise the upper body and can protect against back pain and injury. This can be done at home with simple but effective exercises like press-ups or core-related drills on a fit-ball.

## Training exercises to improve leg strength

### STEP JUMP

- ❑ Stand with feet flat and in line with your hips. Sit back into a squat and spring upwards onto a box, landing gently with bent knees
- ❑ Step down from the box and repeat six to eight times with a rest between each one
- ❑ Good for sprinting power in the legs but should only be done after a month of strength exercises on the legs

### SQUATS

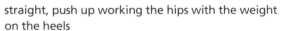

- ❑ Rest bar on neck, not spine, with feet at shoulder width and pointing slightly out
- ❑ Using your core and keeping the back straight, push up working the hips with the weight on the heels
- ❑ Use glutes to push up and lock out the hips in one smooth movement. Make sure you look ahead and remain flat on your feet. Repeat in sets of five starting with just the bar
- ❑ Good for leg and core strength and general stability

### BOX JUMP

- ❑ Use the same technique as the step jump, keeping back straight and landing gently on the ground
- ❑ Only do box and step jumps after a month of leg strength exercises as they can be hard on the legs

### REAR LEG ELEVATED SQUAT

- ❑ Hips facing forward with head up, take a big step on one leg keeping a 90-degree angle in the knee as you slowly lower the other leg until the hip is level with the knee. Feel the glutes and hamstring
- ❑ Slowly come back up taking the weight through the heel and maintaining a straight back. Repeat in sets of five
- ❑ Good strength exercise for legs especially if you have a weak core or back. Also good for strength imbalances in the legs but can be mixed with squats if no back issues

# Planning a training programme

↑ You'll need to train for a cycling holiday in the Alps.

There isn't much point following a training programme without having at least one target event or measurable goal. That's why it's so important that, before you begin training, you've committed to one or more goals at least six to twelve months ahead. It can be further ahead, of course, with stepping-stone targets on the way. Only when you have an idea of the challenge can you plan a suitable programme to bring you up to the desired standard on the day.

A typical range of events for a year of cycling could include some or all of the following:

- 100km (60 miles) sportive in spring at a Level 1 easy pace.
- Training holiday averaging 80–100km (50–60 miles) over seven days, mixed pace from Level 1 to 4 easy–sprint.
- Race or time trial at Level 2–3 brisk–hard pace up to two hours in late spring.
- 160km (100 miles) sportive in early summer at a Level 2 brisk pace.
- 200km (120 miles) all-day ride in summer at Level 1 easy pace.
- All-day summer ride/holiday up and down mountain passes at Level 2–3 brisk–hard pace.
- Multi-day Level 1–2 easy–brisk pace cycling touring holiday in autumn.

Apart from racing, especially shorter events lasting around one hour, most of the challenges above are endurance-based and could be achievable on a surprisingly modest volume of Level 1 and 2 easy and brisk riding. That's how many cyclists get into shape and there's nothing wrong with a relatively unstructured approach based on between five and ten hours a week with one long ride of three to five hours every few weeks.

If you ride regularly in a group of cyclists or your training takes in a lot of hills, the changes of pace in a group and the extra power required for hill-climbing can, almost by default, result in fitness levels high enough for racing.

Riding on 'feel' works for some, but many cyclists prefer to use a more structured and measurable way to work towards their goals. Going confidently into an event in the knowledge that you've hit your targets in training and are, at the very least, capable of finishing at your target level takes the guesswork out of getting into shape.

A coach will always work back from your target events, building up the endurance miles, adding strength and power sessions, always with rest periods in between, before tapering to the event itself. If multiple challenges are planned, you may use one or two as fitness tests towards the number one goal, or you may wish to mix events to suit a periodised training programme sustainable over multiple months or even years.

## Do I need a coach?

A coach can make a massive difference to your cycling and it's well worth investigating if there's one in your area, your club or online, who can provide you with training plans and advice. Don't underestimate the depth of knowledge that an experienced coach can pass on, saving you months if not years of possibly outdated and misinformed advice from well-meaning fellow cyclists.

A good coach will ensure you have the correct bike set-up and kit before you start training seriously and will also coach you on many aspects of riding technique, stressing the importance of cadence and pedalling technique. Above all, for many clients a coach provides the motivation, scrutiny and encouragement they need to follow a training programme in the midst of a busy lifestyle.

# Riding zone effort

## LEVEL 1
### → Easy
Club-run pace when you can talk freely to the rider next to you and the legs are spinning but not aching. Ideally the cadence will be above 80rpm, maintained or even faster on the climbs. This is the pace you can hold for rides over two hours and all day when you're in shape.

*Best for:* Base fitness and endurance, building heart and muscle capacity, switching the body to a leaner burning mix of glycogen and stored fat.

## LEVEL 2
### → Brisk
You're pushing on the pedals at Level 2, aching but not hurting. Conversation isn't so easy as at Level 1 and on short ramps and climbs you may be out of the saddle to hold a steady pace. A two-hour ride at Level 2 would be a regular session for the time-hungry cyclist who can't find the time for half-day rides of three hours plus.

*Best for:* Endurance with some power, growing heart and muscle capacity especially intermediate muscle types in-between slow and fast twitch fibres.

## LEVEL 3
### → Hard
Highest quality training effort, which requires total concentration and can only be sustained for about one hour. Not possible to utter more than a few words here and there. The legs are hurting. Level 3 at the higher end would equate to the effort made during a one-hour time trial over about 25 miles. Just below that is the sweet spot zone of training at Level 3 which would be similar to the big effort you might make towards the end of a sportive.

*Best for:* Going into your functional threshold where aerobic effort morphs into anaerobic. Very good for power as well as endurance but should only be attempted after a base training phase. Raises lactate threshold and maximal lactate steady state pace.

↑ Level 4 is a full-on sprint!

## LEVEL 4
### → Sprint
For sprint riding you can include short intervals up to one minute as well as the shortest bursts of around ten seconds. The effort is total, flat-out at a high cadence above 90rpm. Similar effort to sprinting for a town sign or longer effort sprinting from one group of riders to another in a race or sportive. Legs? screaming!

*Best for:* Power and small increases in VO2 max. Improves cardiac output and utilises the fast twitch muscle fibres.

# Training week

Below is a real-life 'big' training week which, if followed over a period of two or three months, will get you fit enough to comfortably ride 60 miles or 100km. It's based on ten hours' training, which is the maximum a typical enthusiast rider need undertake in any week to achieve an excellent level of fitness. If a ten-hour week isn't possible, try to complete the harder, shorter sessions while cutting back on the long endurance rides. Between five and seven hours' training per week is a realistic target for time-hungry riders – in brackets are ride times to reflect a lighter week of training.

Training to ride 100 miles should involve at least six months using the same schedule, with an easy week in the run-up to the event. For sportives over very hilly routes and racing these training weeks will get you to the finish, but if you're serious about competition, it's worth taking on a coach or at least drawing up a more detailed programme tailored to your strengths and weaknesses and your target events.

### Ten-hour training week (five-hour version in brackets)

| Day | Duration | Session |
| --- | --- | --- |
| Monday | Rest | Ideally the day after the longest ride or an event, add core exercises. |
| Tuesday | 1hr 30min | L2 with L3 for 10min 5x2min at L3. |
| Wednesday | 2hr (rest) | L1 alone or in a group. |
| Thursday | 1hr 30min | L2 competitive group ride with L4 over hilltops and sprints. |
| Friday | Rest | Weights or core exercises. |
| Saturday | 2hr | L2 with hills and L3 for 10min. |
| Sunday | 3hr (rest) | L1 and L2 ideally in a group. |

← If you can't do a ten-hour week, try to increase the intensity of each session.

## Should I shave my legs?

Competitive male cyclists traditionally shave their legs, and many amateurs and just about all professionals continue to do so. Professionals need shaved legs to help with massage and the cleaning and sterilising of road rash. There's a small aerodynamic advantage, but the main reason apart from the reasons above is that it looks good and marks out the rider as a cycling warrior. Most sportive cyclists see no need to shave their legs and in recent times it's become perfectly acceptable, even among older club cyclists, to forego the irksome chore of leg shaving.

# Lifestyle and nutrition

A healthy lifestyle while training helps the body make the most of the break-down-build-up process. You don't have to live like a monk but there are two key factors that will contribute to achieving your fitness goals.

Training stresses the body. Sleep allows it to recover, repair and adapt for the next session. The body reacts to the stress of training by coming back stronger to handle that stress, but if you don't give it a chance to rest and repair the training effect will be lessened and symptoms of overtraining can manifest themselves. It can even lead to injury and ill health.

After sleep the other pillar of your healthy cycling lifestyle is nutrition. Avoiding junk food, moderating your intake of alcohol and switching your diet to a low carb one with more protein, fat and plant-based foodstuffs isn't only beneficial to your general health, it'll also encourage your body to switch from a glucose to a fat-burning machine.

## Sleep
Getting at least seven hours a night is ideal time for the body to repair the damage done to the muscles in training.

## Nutrition
- Cut down on 'quick sugar' high GI carbs like mash/baked potatoes and chips, white pasta/bread, chocolate and cakes.
- Eat moderate volumes of 'slow sugar' low GI carbs like oats, pulses and wholemeal pasta/bread.

↑ Eating healthily will help the body to benefit from efforts on the bike.

- Have more vegetable on the plate than anything else and go for dark green veg such as kale, broccoli, spinach and winter greens.
- Superfoods for recovery and anti-oxidants include beetroot, blueberries and cherry juice.
- Protein foods include eggs, fish, lean meat, beans, lentils, pulses, yoghurt, cheese, milk and nuts.

↓ Low GI carbs include oats, pulses and wholemeal pasta or bread.

## On-bike fuel

Hydration is the most important fuelling consideration when you're out riding. It's widely accepted that staying hydrated is important even in normal daily life. When taking exercise it becomes even more essential. In hot weather fluid loss on the bike can be as high as one litre per hour, which is the equivalent of two cycling bottles.

Cyclists sweat like any other athletes but the cooling and drying effect of the wind, especially in winter, can fool them into thinking they're not becoming dehydrated. Even on the shortest rides of an hour or so a bottle of water should be carried on the bike, and finished by the time the ride's over. If dual bottle cages are fitted it's worth taking two bottles on rides over two hours, or refilling a single bottle at a shop.

Water's fine for most rides and it's easier to keep the bottles clean if it isn't mixed with anything sugary. If it's hot or the ride's a competitive event or race then it may be necessary to fill the bottles with an electrolyte or carb mix.

## Eating on the bike

For longer rides from two hours upwards it may be necessary to eat while in the saddle. Most sportives have a couple of feeding stations where riders can stop and take on anything from Jelly Babies to flapjacks and savoury biscuits. If you're racing or not doing an organised ride, some food must be carried with you and consumed on the go.

↓ Sportives have feed stations where you can fuel up on carbs and drink.

↑ Always carry a bottle on every ride, even if it's just water, and finish it before the end of the ride.

Ideally it's best to snack on natural products like bananas or dried fruit, but it's hard to ignore the huge choice of sports energy bars and gels that can be popped into a pocket and taste almost as good. Energy bars can be bought in bulk online or individually in bike shops and supermarkets. Gels are more sports-specific and should only be used sparingly, at the end of a ride for instance, as multiple gels can upset your stomach.

If you're training for a long event, it pays to practise with different bars and gels to find the ones you like best and then ensure those are the ones you use on the big day.

## Signs of overtraining

**Too much riding or, more likely, cramming in the training around a busy lifestyle can lead to symptoms of overtraining. If you should notice these occurring it's best to take a week off, then return to low levels of training until you feel energised again. You'll also need to assess whether your overtrained state was due to an exceptionally busy time in your life, or had been building up over time due to cramming too much in. If it's the latter then you may need to take a longer, harder look at how cycling fits into your life, and possibly find ways to train smarter, using up less time.**

### SYMPTOMS OF OVERTRAINING

- **Always feeling tired.**
- **Persistently sore muscles.**
- **Irritable, grumpy and frustrated.**
- **Sleeping too much/too little.**
- **Elevated or suppressed heart rate.**
- **Picking up colds, viruses and skin lesions.**
- **No zip, on the bike or anywhere else!**

# Pedalling technique

An efficient, fluid pedal stroke at cadences from around 70 to 110rpm is the key technique to master in cycling. Using the correct technique will ensure you train more effectively as well as earn respect from fellow cyclists, and turning the cranks quickly and smoothly is an extremely satisfying sensation. It's right at the heart of what distinguishes a bike rider from a cyclist and is the reason pedalling is considered by connoisseurs to be a kinetic art form.

Transmitting power to the back wheel is how the bicycle is propelled. When you consider that the average bike rider produces about 0.25hp and even a top road cyclist only averages 0.5hp when riding hard, it's no surprise cyclists care so much about eking out the maximum Watts in the most efficient way. (746W = 1hp and 1W = 0.0013hp.)

The higher an internal combustion engine revs the more power it makes. The shrieking ear-splitting sound of a Formula One engine is down to its incredibly high-revving motor, its banks of lightweight pistons going up and down at up to 15,000 revs, producing 600hp from an engine no bigger than a basic saloon car's. A cyclist has just two pistons doing the same job as a petrol engine, and although it's very important to develop a fast cadence it isn't a case of revving to stratospheric levels like an F1 motor.

⬇ **Developing a brisk, efficient and stylish cadence is one the great pleasures and challenges of cycling.**

A match sprinter on the track or a rider competing in a roller competition may hit 160rpm for a burst of power up to 2,000W for no more than a minute or so, but raised oxygen uptake and an elevated heart rate make pedalling over 110rpm something that only a well trained cyclist can sustain for sustained periods.

Think of cadence as the equivalent of lifting a weight. A light weight can be raised and lowered many times with speed and dexterity for a long time, resulting in a high figure for the total weight lifted. A heavy weight can be heaved back and forth a few times but the exertion for each lift is greater and fatigue sets in sooner. The mass of the weight is also harder to control, with a greater risk of injury if the technique is flawed. Pedalling follows the same principle; in a smaller gear the rider can pedal faster for longer, producing higher power outputs as well as maintaining the ability to make multiple accelerations without 'blowing up'.

For road-racing and interval training a fast cadence is imperative, as you'll be left behind in short order in the crazy changes of pace of a road race, and for short intervals it's vital to be able to accelerate quickly to the required level.

## Ideal cadence

Between 70 and 110rpm is the most efficient rev band. About 90rpm is ideal, as it balances muscle stress against oxygen uptake and heart rate. It's easy to count your pedal strokes. To note your

cadence just find a flat piece of road and for 30 seconds count one each time one foot reaches the 12 o'clock position. Double it, and that's your revs per minute. After a while you get to know how fast you're pedalling by how it feels. Power meters and on-bike sensors can also measure and display cadence in real time.

## Crank length

Shorter cranks suit higher cadences, which is partly why track bikes are fitted with cranks that are 165mm long. On a single fixed-gear track bike the only way to produce more power is to rev ever faster, and shorter cranks reduce the 'windmill' effect of the legs, allowing them to pump up and down more efficiently. Riders with shorter legs can pedal cranks that are 165mm or 170mm on the road to good effect. Average-height males will normally be suited to 172.5mm cranks, with taller riders sometimes favouring 175mm cranks.

## The power stroke

With the feet attached securely to clip-in pedals it's tempting to pull up as well as push down, making full use of the complete pedal revolution. For many years it was assumed that pulling up, 'pushing' the knee towards the bars at the top of the pedal stroke and then 'pawing' at the very bottom of the stroke, was the best technique for pedalling.

Tests on elite riders, however, showed that when they were pedalling hard very little if any upward pressure was applied on the up, top and bottom of the pedal stroke. In fact, all it indicated was that the rider was merely helping to unload his foot in order to return it as efficiently as possible to the power phase.

The sweet spot for pedalling power starts just after the pedal commences its downward stroke and continues no further than

↑ Longer cranks may suit a rider over six feet tall with long legs.

the five o'clock position. Maximum power is applied when the knee is directly above the pedal, which should correspond to the three o'clock position when the pedal's horizontal to the ground.

When pedalling this way at around 90rpm the power phases come around very quickly on each side and it isn't necessary at all to try and pull up on the pedals. On the upstroke side the leg is rested, allowing the rider to get the most efficient transfer of power when the cranks return to the one o'clock position.

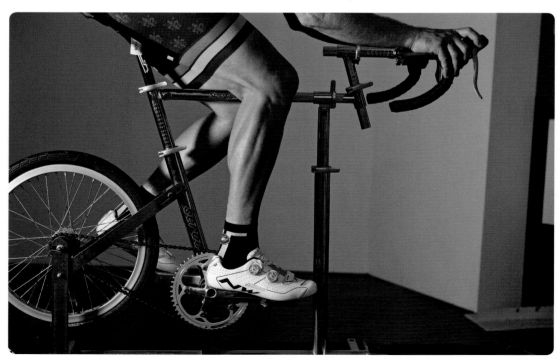

← Maximum power is applied when the knee is directly above the pedal with the cranks horizontal to the ground.

# Turbo training benefits

Nothing beats the turbo trainer for a short, quality workout designed to improve a specific aspect of your cycling. Turbo training interval sessions are particularly effective for increasing power and threshold riding (Level 3) as well as working on your VO2 max and ability to sprint (Level 4). Cadence drills will also greatly benefit your road riding.

Turbo training at home or as part of an organised session at a gym has become a regular part of many cyclists' weekly sessions no matter the season. Gone are the days when the turbo was reluctantly dragged from the shed as the only alternative to a cancelled mid-winter ride.

Modern turbos are quiet and come close to replicating the feel of pedalling a bike on the open road. Bike-, body- or turbo-mounted sensors and computers can show power, heart rate and cadence and can also be programmed with interval sessions and, if there's a screen, virtual scenarios such as a race or mountain climb. A weekly turbo session can be a great way to focus your quality training effort into a block of time as short as 30 minutes. For time-hungry riders a short session can be completed in the lunch hour or at either end of the day.

While there's nothing to stop you doing a steady-paced Level 2 turbo ride for multiple hours there aren't many cyclists who can put up with the monotony and if at all possible it's much more enjoyable to get out on the road for long endurance rides. Motivation and variety is key to getting the most from turbo training and if you approach a session with a sinking feeling you'll soon start to find ways of bunking off!

## Your max heart rate (MHR)

It's possible to perform interval sessions on the turbo on 'feel' or perceived exertion, as described by the Levels 1–4 on pages 135, but after power the best way to monitor effort is with a heart rate monitor. Many turbo sessions use percentages of max heart rate, which takes the guesswork out of following a session.

To find your maximum heart rate warm up on the turbo for ten minutes then, in a higher gear, gradually increase the revs until the final minute when you should be sprinting flat out at your maximum revs for the final 20 seconds. During that final effort your heart rate should hit its maximum and be recorded on the monitor. Change down into a lower gear and spin the pedals for at least another five minutes until you feel you've recovered from the effort.

Only do a max heart rate effort when you're feeling rested and fresh. If you find it tough to increase your heart rate during the warm-up you may be tired or unwell, so throttle off and leave it for another day.

↓ Turbo training can be the most effective way to work on cadence as well as quality intervals.

# Four popular turbo-training sessions

All these sessions should begin with 5–10 minutes warm-up on an easy gear, building up to a cadence of 100 with a couple of sprints thrown in. By the time you start the session for real you should be sweating freely and breathing deeply.

## Turbo training tips

**It's best not to turbo train near bedtime as it can take a few hours to come down from a high intensity effort.**

**Turbo training makes you hot and sweaty. Wear cycling shorts and a thin undervest. Drape a towel over the bars to catch sweat and mop your brow. Have a drink ready nearby too.**

↓ Your turbo training kit should include a towel and something to drink.

## 1 Training ride

If road riding is impossible, this is a session that can take its place. Between each segment, ride easily in a low gear for five minutes. Build up the intensity as the session progresses by maintaining a cadence of 80–100rpm but changing up the gears to increase the resistance. Total ride time is up to you but it can be as long as 2hr 30min.

- 55min at 65–79% MHR.
- 40min at 70–75% MHR.
- 25min at 75–80% MHR.
- 10min at 80–85% MHR.

## 2 Threshold

A hard one-hour session the equivalent of Level 3, which would be similar to just above time-trial effort. Only do this when you're feeling rested and fresh and after a longer than usual warm-up. Put in five minutes' easy riding between each hard segment.

- 10min at 75–80% MHR.
- 2x5min at 80–85% MHR with 1min easy in between.
- 3x2min at 85–90% MHR with 30sec easy in between.
- 6x1min at 90–95% MHR with 30sec easy in between.

## 3 Sprint

A 35min session that's great for short full-throttle efforts. Pedalling should be at least 80rpm in a gear with reasonable resistance. Concentrate on holding your pedalling technique and not moving your upper body. Can be added to a regular ride turbo session or after a good warm-up.

- 15sec at 100% MHR sprint.
- 2min 45sec recovery after each sprint.
- Repeat up to 10 times with 5min recovery between each.

## 4 Steps

Short but hard and full-on. Like the sprint session so could be added to another turbo session of moderate intensity. Great for leg speed and top end. If you do more than one set, add five minutes' easy riding in between.

- 15sec sprint with 45sec easy.
- 30sec sprint with 30sec easy.
- 45sec sprint with 15sec easy.
- 60sec sprint with 60sec easy.
- 45sec sprint with 15sec easy.
- 30sec sprint with 30sec easy.
- 15sec sprint with 45sec easy.

# Bike handling

Being in control of the bike won't only make you a safer cyclist, it'll greatly enhance your enjoyment of every ride. There's nothing like feeling at one with the machine as you lean it over through a corner or tuck-in on a fast descent. Riding out of the saddle is also very satisfying but can take some practice before it comes naturally. Learning how to brake hard without locking the wheels is another skill that cyclists never stop trying to perfect.

Road bikes, even budget models, are light machines compared to mountain bikes or hybrids, and the transition from fat tyres to skinny ones can be unnerving. A road bike feels lively, with quick steering and a firm ride that transmits every rough patch and jolt through the bars and saddle.

One of the first things a road rider learns is how to scan the road ahead and weave around unwelcome patches and potholes. Everyone hits a pothole from time to time – the best outcome is to see it and react fast enough to prevent a puncture, damage to the wheel or, at the very worst, a crash.

After a few rides on a road bike most riders thrill to the extra feedback and responsiveness compared to an MTB. Not only do you go faster for the same level of effort, but a road bike will transport you all day in comfort.

Lack of confidence is one the biggest factors contributing to people giving up cycling, as it's no fun feeling vulnerable when riding in traffic, in the wet or at speed along twisty

↑ Mastering skills like riding out of the saddle will make you a faster and safer rider.

↓ Learn to scan the road ahead for potholes or gravel.

roads. So mastering the basics of bike handling should be high on your to-do list if you're new to cycling. Most of us learned to cycle as children, so at least we know how to stay upright, steer and brake.

The basics are enough to get you out on the road but you'll be a much safer and faster rider if you treat bike handling as a continual learning process which rewards technique and a calm head far more than relying on reactions and bravado.

Another element of bike handling is roadcraft. Cycling takes place on public roads and often in company with other cyclists. Cyclists not only need to have knowledge of and obey the rules of the road but should also have an appreciation of how the activity of cycling affects other road users as well as their fellow cyclists. Staying safe in motorised traffic is the absolute priority of roadcraft, but at a more advanced level the skills and etiquette of group riding, drafting and racing tactics also come into play.

↑ Confidence makes all the difference when riding in traffic or on wet roads.

↓ Roadcraft takes your basic skills to another level, especially when riding in a group.

# Safety first

Cyclists ride mostly on the open road, mixing with other traffic and contending with hazards common to the everyday road user. Bike riders are more aware than other road users of the painful consequences of a crash and are used to a higher level of vigilance and concentration. That's the first rule of the road – stay alert at all times, because when you switch off that's when mistakes occur.

Don't just rely on your eyes either, use all your senses – listen out for traffic and sniff out the road and climactic conditions. Try to scan the road a few metres ahead as you ride along, to give yourself time to steer around rough patches and potholes. The faster you go, the further ahead you need to look.

Remember that in most situations involving traffic you're the most vulnerable road user and need to ride defensively, thinking further ahead than usual and always giving yourself time and space to steer or brake yourself out of danger. Don't rely on your reactions – it's much better to anticipate a hazard and get used to a series of actions that can be performed repeatedly. On the few occasions when you're genuinely taken by surprise your chances of coming away unscathed are much higher if your avoidance process automatically kicks in.

Feeling confident on the bike is vital. Try the following things when out riding and when it's safe to do so.

## Potholes

Switch around a pothole by keeping the bike upright and turning the bars quite quickly one way then back to the straight ahead. You'll be surprised how rapidly the machine can be made to dart around a small obstacle. If you do ride into a pothole all you can do is unload the handlebars to try and reduce the force of the impact of the tyre against the sides of the hole. If you lessen your grip on the bars and shift your weight rearwards you can avoid puncturing or damaging the wheel.

It's worth practicing a 'bunny hop' on the bike, as the ability to jump a bike – especially when riding at speed – can be safer than making a last-second change of direction. It's easy to hop

the bike when you're using clip-in pedals. Simultaneously pull up on the bars and pedals while riding in a straight line and with your bum out of the saddle. You only need a few inches of air beneath your tyres to clear a small hole. At speed the bike will travel further and clear a bigger obstacle.

↓ A bunny hop can lift the bike just far enough off the ground to clear a small pothole.

### Bike fit

A correctly fitting bike that allows you to sit comfortably within reach of all the controls without feeling stretched or cramped is essential for confident bike handling. A session with a professional bike fitter is worth every penny if you come away knowing that your machine has been set up correctly for comfort and ease of handling. See Chapter 5 for bike fit advice.

↑ In wet conditions do everything smoothly and trust your tyres!

## Braking

It's surprising how hard you can brake on a road bike, especially on bikes with 25c or fatter tyres and quality front brakes, either traditional caliper or disc. The front brake is more effective than the rear, which will lock much earlier. Practise braking progressively harder on the front brake than on the rear. In the wet, braking force can be 50:50.

## Wet weather

Concentrate on doing everything extra-smoothly if the roads are wet. Primarily that means braking earlier and less forcefully than you would normally, especially with caliper brakes, which need to clear water from the rim before reaching full power.

All braking should be completed before leaning the bike over for a corner, and in the corner itself the angle of lean is smaller than in the dry. Keep everything smooth, relaxed and predictable in the wet and you shouldn't have any slides or crashes. Quality road tyres with excellent grip characteristics make all the difference too.

## Listen and sniff

Listen out for traffic approaching from behind – with practice it's possible to distinguish how close behind it is and if it's slowing down or moving out to go around you. Lorries and diesel vans are especially worth noting. There may not be much you can do about traffic approaching from behind but sometimes you can pull in closer to the verge or wave them past if the road is clear ahead.

Get used to the sound your tyres make, as they can give away clues as to the road surface – especially if there's gravel about. A crunching sound or gravel pinging off the down tube is a warning that you may be on unstable ground.

Diesel is very slippery and is usually spilled from overfilled trucks on roundabouts. You can see the dark stain on the road and you can also often smell it in time to be on high alert. Other hazards that can be anticipated by smell are cow pats on the road, damp patches under trees and the pungent smell of freshly laid tarmac.

## The safe bike

Ensure your brakes are working as efficiently as possible, with smoothly running cables and quality brake blocks. Even budget brake calipers can be improved greatly by a set of quality replacement brake blocks. Make sure you can comfortably reach and operate the brake levers when riding on the hoods and on the drops of the handlebars. Your arms should be bent when you're braking as that'll help to absorb any bumps.

Take care of your tyres. Check the pressures before every ride with a track pump and gauge and replace them if they become excessively worn or damaged. Buy the best tyres you can afford as they'll offer more grip and feedback than budget options.

→ Quality tyres at the correct pressures offer better grip and feedback than budget options.

## SAFETY DOS AND DON'TS

- DO ride defensively but with confidence, especially in town.
- DO take up your rightful position on the road, but try to let traffic overtake when it's safe to do so.
- DO obey stop signals and pull-up off the road where you won't hold up traffic.
- DON'T assume that because you ride a bike you can do whatever you like.
- DON'T expect other road users to do the right thing – always anticipate a hazardous scenario.
- DON'T go looking for trouble, as if you do you'll always find it.

# Cornering

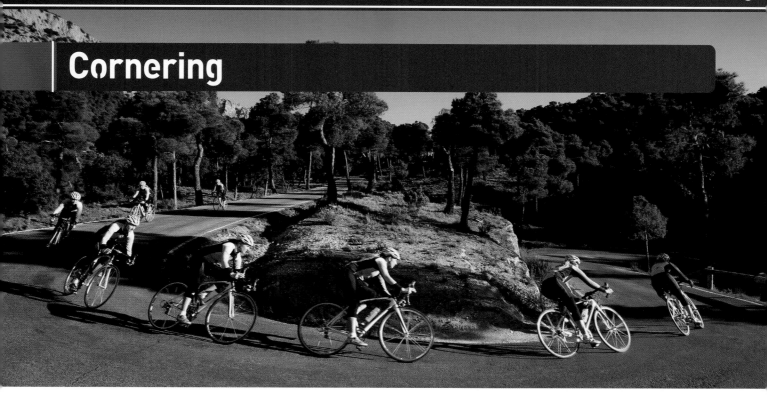

A cyclist who knows how to corner quickly and safely can take a few metres or seconds from a less skilled rider on every bend. If you're that slower rider you'll be playing catch-up on fast corners in the flat or down every twisting descent. You'll be sprinting to catch up while your better-handling friend takes a breather waiting for you.

Taking corners quickly is often seen as a test of bravery and little more. It doesn't help that words like 'fearless' and 'crazy' are attached to faster riders in a group when in fact those riders are often the ones using handling techniques and strategies that make them safer than the riders they leave far behind on the downhills.

Looking ahead far enough to define the type of corner is the most important technique to learn, as well as understanding why the apex is so important. The other key elements to cornering are road position, leaning over and braking.

## Apex

If you were to draw an imaginary line showing the smoothest and therefore quickest line through a corner, the point at which the line passes closest to the inside of the bend is called the apex. On a perfect curve the apex will be at the tip of the curve, but most bends aren't perfect and the apex moves to one side or the other of the radius depending on how 'closed' or 'open' the exit to the corner is.

On a closed road or circuit the apex can be clipped every time, with the rider using every inch of the ideal line around the corner just like you'd see in a closed-circuit F1 or Moto GP race. On the open road the apex will still be the point at which the rider comes closest to the inside of the corner but road conditions and other traffic will determine how closely the racing line can be followed.

↑ Cornering is a technique that can be learned and endlessly honed. It's a lot of fun too.

## Look up!

When you're cycling quickly towards a corner it pays to keep your head up and to look as far forward 'into' the bend as you can. You're looking at the point where the road disappears from sight, and it'll appear to you as a tapered, up-ended V. This is the called the vanishing point, and if the tip of the V continues to move as you approach the entrance to the corner, smoothly opening up the sightline as you lean the bike into the bend, you're in a fast corner and can carry all your speed through the bend.

If the vanishing point appears not to be moving or is moving very slowly the bend is tightening, and you need to gently apply the brakes until the exit opens up.

↓ The apex is where the ideal line through a corner comes closest to touching the inside edge of the bend.

↑ Watch any experienced rider and they'll be looking up and 'through' the corner.

Looking up and ahead is crucial as the principle for driving is the same for cycling – look where you want to go and the machine will follow.

## Types of bend

Some bends can catch you out and for that reason you should always keep something in reserve either under braking or in the lean angle deployed.

A constant-radius bend describes a smooth arc with open sightlines on the entrance and exit and with the apex located in the centre of the inside of the bend. This is the fastest bend you can encounter and can usually be dispatched with little more than a change of lean angle.

↓ It's fine to follow the lines of experienced riders on descents but you should never feel pressured into it.

A hairpin bend may have a fairly constant radius but it's too tight to take without braking and a fair amount of lean angle. If possible take a wide line into the bend, either in the centre of the road or on the far side if the road is closed. The bend can be apexed further around as the bike is leant through the corner but on the open road it's best to play safe and brake to a much slower speed until the vanishing point begins to open and you can pedal through the exit. If in doubt repeat 'in slow, out fast' as you approach tight downhill hairpin bends.

A blind bend doesn't reveal its exit until you're deep into the corner and all you can do is brake well into the turn with care until the corner opens up. Not much lean angle can be carried in the first half of the corner.

A dual radius corner can catch you out, as it effectively has two apexes with a middle bend section. Consequently it's a tricky corner to get around as it has two vanishing points. As with all corners, if you keep your head up and train your eyes on the vanishing point it'll greatly help to maintain safe and smooth progress through the bend.

## Lean the bike

A moving bike changes direction by leaning, not steering in the conventional sense. The bike turns thanks to a process called counter-steering, which is something we all do subconsciously and which actually involves turning the bars very slightly away from the desired direction of travel. This causes the machine to lean over and take the intended line.

When turning the bike through fast corners or on descents keep your body completely still and let your straightened outside leg take a little of the weight off your behind. You don't have to kick the inside knee out, as it's more important to feel at one with the bike with the balance distributed equally for and aft.

# Roadcraft

↑ Riding in a well-drilled and compact group, like a breakaway in a road race, is a key component of cycling roadcraft.

Once you've learned the basics of bike handling the next bike-riding challenge comes when you start riding with other cyclists. Some riders find this nerve-wracking, which is hardly surprising, as going from solo riding to having even one other cyclist within a few inches can take a while to get used to.

Why ride along close to other cyclists at all? Many cyclists have no wish to ride too close to other bike riders, either because they find it's too risky or because they don't want to be knocked off by someone they don't trust. Fair enough, but there are three reasons why every cyclist should at least consider group riding.

## 1 Drafting
Riding behind another cyclist saves a significant amount of energy, up to 40% if you're nestled in a group riding over 20mph. Wind resistance is by far the biggest force to overcome when cycling. At 25mph about 90% of your effort is expended just pushing against the air, so if you ride a bike-length or less behind another cyclist you can save a lot of energy. Drafting underpins just about every bike racing tactic and explains why competitive cycling is so intriguing to watch.

→ Sitting directly behind another cyclist is a perfectly acceptable way to make life easier for yourself.

### Is it wrong to draft?
Blame triathlon for making drafting a punishable offence (which they have now dropped), but no cyclist should feel embarrassed if they sit behind another rider for whatever reason they like. 'Sitting in the wheels' is a time-honoured cycling tradition – if you don't like it happening to you, speed up!

## 2 Safety

A group of cyclists riding in a compact formation is easier for a motorist to pass than a straggling line of riders spread over three or four times the distance. Cars trying to pass individual riders end up being frustrated and weaving dangerously in and out between individual cyclists. In a tight-knit group riding two abreast traffic can pass quickly and safely. Even if the group singles up the riders should try not to let more than a bike-length gap open up between each them.

## 3 Sociability

Riding in a group is fun and can be very sociable. Two cyclists can ride alongside each other and if they're close enough can have a normal conversation lasting as long as the ride itself. In a bigger group ride if the riders are rotating, there's a chance to talk to numerous folk – even if you're just passing the time of day it makes the ride go by much quicker.

## How to ride in a group

Get used to 'sitting on the wheel' by going out with a trusted and experienced cyclist who you know will ride at a steady pace and point out hazards as you go along. Start off half a bike-length behind and work your way right up to the rear tyre of the bike in front. Stay relaxed and very lightly brush the brakes to adjust your speed. Think about where the wind is coming from and use all your guile to get as much shelter as possible.

You'll be surprised how much less energy you need when you follow closely behind another cyclist, even to the point where you may be freewheeling when the rider in front is still pedalling along.

↓ A long line of cyclists forces traffic to weave in and out over a much longer stretch than if the cyclists are in a compact group.

→ Riding in a group involves collaborating with the other members to share the pace-making in a safe, smoothly working zone.

When you're confident that you can sit on a wheel you can try riding in a small group, getting used to having a rider alongside and in front. Don't panic if you touch elbows – bikes are stable machines that won't fall over if you occasionally bump an elbow or handlebar.

The generally accepted guidelines for riding in a group are as follows:

- Whether it's you and a friend or you're one of dozens in a fast-moving bunch, the principles of group riding are the same.
- Ride two-abreast, with the leading two riders looking out for hazards and pointing them out to anyone behind.
- Ride in a tight-knit formation, directly alongside the rider next to you and almost touching elbows. Try not to continually ride half a wheel ahead of the rider alongside – 'half-wheeling' is considered bad practice!
- Don't continually overlap your front wheel with the rear wheel of the rider in front. If that rider swerves it could take you out as well.
- In a group of four or more riding two abreast you should expect to do a turn on the front now and again. Going 'through and off' is a very enjoyable process, best learned with experienced group riders who'll show you how to pull off and join the rear of the group, leaving the pair in second place at the front.
- When riding in a group do everything smoothly and predictably, especially if it's a 'breakaway' group sharing the pace-making at the front. The objective is to maintain a steady pace at all times, not to accelerate or slow down when it's your turn at the front.

# Hazard warnings

When cyclists ride in a group or draft behind one another, the rider behind can't always see potential hazards in the road ahead. If the rider in front swerves to avoid a pothole, for instance, the rider behind could plough into it with damaging results.

Cyclists expect to be warned by the rider in front, who should point down at the road indicating the side the pothole is on, or make a sweeping wave behind his or her back to indicate a parked car or obstacle in the road. When riding in country lanes it's also helpful to warn other riders if a car approaches in front or behind. Usually a shout of 'car up' or 'car down' will suffice, giving everyone time to give the car room to pass.

Group riding on the road is different to solo cycling. You become part of an informal team whenever you ride with others and it's everyone's responsibility to communicate with each other and look out for potential hazards on behalf of the group.

→ Use hand signals to indicate hazards ahead or in the road, such as parked cars and potholes.

# CHAPTER 7
# SPORTIVES AND RACING

There are many ways to test your fitness or have a go at competition. No matter your age or ability there are rides and events in which you can time yourself, race others side-by-side or achieve a finishing position. A certificate and finisher's medal in a sportive is something to be proud of, and taking part in any form of road competition takes admirable levels of determination and commitment.

Twenty years ago the most popular way to ride with other cyclists either competitively or socially was with a cycling club. Most young cyclists would join a club and straight away find themselves riding in groups of all ages and competing in grassroots competition like short circuit road races and club time trials over ten miles. These days the average age of a new rider is higher and they're more likely to ride as a non-club member, gaining their first serious experience of group riding in a sportive or challenge event.

Levels of fitness gained from sportives can certainly be high enough for racing and no one should be put off the step up to serious competition and racing. It remains the case, however, that joining a club helps enormously in terms of the amount of help and advice on hand.

↓ **There's a competitive cycling event for every type of road cyclist.**

# Sportives

Mass participation rides, some with many thousands of riders, are the most popular form of competition in cycling today. While not strictly speaking races, sportives are timed events over set distances with every entrant recording a finishing time and often his or her overall position. Times and positions can even be age- and gender-related, adding to the appeal of sportives to every level of rider.

There's no requirement for a licence to ride a sportive, most of which are run by independent organisations either for profit or on behalf of a charity. Entering an event is usually a simple matter of registering online and paying the entrance fee. After that all you need to do is prepare for the big day with a suitable training programme.

On the day riders are sent off in groups, which could be composed of riders all going for the same distance option or according to their predicted finishing time. Once under way there's no obligation to ride with your group – you can drop back or surge ahead riding solo or in smaller groups if you like. That's the attraction for many – you can choose whether to ride in a pack or alone or both.

A sportive is a great way to do a half or full day of riding as hard as you can around a safe signposted route with feed stations and technical support. The presence of other riders adds an element of competition as well as company. Every cycling nation has a sportive scene with famous events based either on historic pro bike race routes or through challenging and hilly terrain.

Multi-day sportives are also growing in popularity, especially for riders looking for a longer challenge often in a foreign country. London to Paris is one of the best known, with rides taking place through the season along the 300-mile (483km)

→ You can ride a sportive on your own, with friends or in a big group.

route. Riders can choose from 24-hour to five-day itineraries depending on fitness, and there's often a charity element. More serious in terms of terrain are the multi-day Haute Route challenges which take place in the Alps, Pyrenees, Dolomites and US Rockies.

Here are just a few of the biggest one-day sportives (also known as 'cyclosportif' or 'gran fondo') events in the world:

### L'Étape du Tour (France)

The Étape takes part in July on one of the stages of the current year's Tour de France, usually in the Alps or Pyrenees. Roads are closed and entrants number 15,000.

### Cape Town Cycle Tour (South Africa)

Billed as the largest timed bike ride in the world, the Cape Town event attracts 35,000 entrants and follows the same closed roads 109km route around Table Mountain every March.

### Ride London–Surrey 100 (UK)

A legacy event from the 2012 Olympic Games in London, the headline event over a weekend of cycling is a closed roads sportive over 100 miles taking in the Olympic road-race climb of Box Hill.

### Tour of Flanders Cyclo (Belgium)

Following some or all of the legendary Flemish classic pro race, the Cyclo offers three routes, all taking in the fabled cobbled 'monts' of the region, and ridden by 16,000 enthusiastic pedallers.

### Gran Fondo Maratona dles Dolomites (Italy)

A July sportive in the heart of the Italian Dolomites with 10,000 entrants tackling routes of 106km and 138km over some of the toughest climbs, including the Passo Sella, Campolongo and Giau.

← Experience the notorious cobbled climbs of Belgium in the Tour of Flanders sportive

## Quebrantahuesos (Spain)

Spain's popular gran fondo in June offers two distances (85km and 200km) and climbs through the Pyrenees into France and back. Entry is by lottery ballot so it's best to have a plan B.

## La Marmotte (France)

The original tough French alpine cyclosportif follows the same 170km route every July and includes the climbs of the Glandon, Galibier and Alpe d'Huez in 5,000m of climbing. Sells out 7,000 places.

## Amstel Gold Race Sportive (Holland)

With six distance options from 60km to the full pro race route of 240km, the Amstel sportive takes place in Holland's hilly Limburg region and finishes on the famous Cauberg climb.

## Paris-Roubaix Challenge (France)

For fans of the notorious cobbled lanes of northern France there are three distances up to 170km taking in the short but brutal cobbled 'sectors' of the great race which takes place the following day in early April.

↓ Retro bikes and gear put the fun into Eroica rides across Europe.

## Audax

One of the hardest challenge rides of all is the historic Paris–Brest–Paris (PBP), a 1,200km randonée organised under the rules of the Audax association. Riders must qualify for the PBP by riding audax events in their own nations from 200km to 600km. The PBP must be completed inside 90 hours and is as much a physical as mental challenge due to the lack of sleep and sheer distance. Audax events are sportives in their most basic form with 100km normally the shortest option.

## Eroica (Italy)

The original retro sportive has inspired similar Eroica events all over Europe and takes place on Tuscany's white gravel roads every October. Period dress and bikes of pre-1987 vintage only.

## Levi's King Ridge Gran Fondo (USA)

This Northern California sportive starts and finishes in Santa Rosa every October and features plenty of scenic climbs along its 160km route.

# Road racing

From the Tour de France to a one-hour circuit race, road racing is the hardest, most competitive and historic form of cycle sport. Set two cyclists off together and at the end of the ride one of them will try to put a wheel ahead of the other as they reach their destination. Put 200 riders on the road with a finishing line 120 miles away, TV moto cameras and helicopters, and you've got a stage of the Tour de France. The effect is the same, just a heck of a lot more entertaining.

Mass-start road racing is as simple as sport gets. As long as you don't take a short cut or knock another rider off his or her bike, the objective is to cross the line first. Times and speeds are irrelevant; winning is everything. Sounds simple doesn't it? But when you take into account the unique dynamics of the bicycle, the advantages of drafting, and how the collective power of teamwork can shape a race, road racing appeals on many fascinating levels. In fact it's a sport where tactics play a massive part and in which a canny rider can finish ahead of stronger rivals on a regular basis.

To enter a road race you'll need a licence issued by the national body which will include third-party insurance.

↓ **Road racing is the ultimate test of fitness and tactics.**

## How to win a road race
### ➜ Sprint!
A high standard of fitness, competent handling and the ability to ride in a pack of riders is enough to finish in the bunch in a road race. Using bike-handling skills and guile it's possible to freewheel inside a bunch of fast-moving riders, leaving the hard work to the riders on the front. On the climbs you'll have to ride as hard as everyone else and if the field fragments you may have to go 'full gas' to close a gap to the bike in front.

By conserving your energy better than everyone else in the pack, and if the race stays together until 150m or so from the line, it's possible to win a race with the fastest finishing sprint. 'Field' sprinters win many races this way.

### ➜ Solo
A single rider attacking and riding away from the bunch is one of the most inspiring sights in cycling. The solo breakaway is the hardest way to win a race, because one cyclist shouldn't in theory outperform two, let alone dozens. But it can succeed, and while the odds are stacked against a solo move there are good tactical arguments in its favour.

Most successful is a solo attack in the final few miles of a race,

when the attacking rider can surprise the bunch and then ride at his or her maximum to the line. At the end of a race everyone is tired and teamwork in the bunch only has to falter for a few minutes for the solo rider to build a winning gap. Solo attacks can also succeed if there's a crash in the bunch; the roads are narrow and technical, favouring the solo rider, and if the bunch underestimates the power of the rider it won't react until it's too late.

↑ If the race finishes in a big bunch you'll need a strong sprint to win.

There's no more emphatic or satisfying way to win a race but it's also the hardest way, demanding absolute commitment, perfect timing, strength and self-belief to pull it off.

↓ Only the strongest riders can hold off the bunch for a solo victory.

⬆ **Riders in a breakaway work together to gain an advantage on the bunch.**

### ➜ Breakaway

If two or more riders escape the bunch the resulting breakaway group can stay ahead if all or most of the riders share pace-making duties. Once a winning advantage over the main field has been established the race can be decided by the members of the break, significantly improving each rider's odds of winning. In an effective working break all the riders go 'through and off' in a smooth, compact formation. Each rider need spend no more than a few seconds on the front before swinging off to allow the rider behind to come through, and so on. Non-sprinters and strong solo riders favour breakaway groups as they can leave the sprinters languishing in the bunch and use their power to drive along the break or make a late solo attack.

## Closed-circuit road racing

A one-hour road race on a closed short circuit is a popular way to experience mass-start competition for the first time. There are purpose-built cycling circuits all over the UK as well as parks and motor-racing circuits where regular events are held. Thanks to the short duration of these races, there can be multiple events for a wide range of abilities and age groups. Groups set off in handicaps are also often smaller and less intimidating than one big bunch.

➜ **Races on closed circuits are safer and often shorter than road racing on the open road.**

# Time trials

Many cycling clubs in the UK hold club and 'open' time trials, which can be from 10 to 100 miles or even 12 or 24 hours. Time trialling used to be the biggest branch of the sport in the UK, introducing young cyclists to timed racing over a set distance, but today young riders are just as likely to ride a sportive, closed-circuit road race, or a track or cyclo-cross event. But time trialling remains the most accessible grass-roots competition. Triathletes also enjoy the individual effort of a time trial, which comes close to the cycling element of a triathlon.

Racing against the watch is a test of speed, pacing and concentration. The appeal for many is that whatever their age or ability they can record a time which can be compared to other competitors or to previously recorded times over the same course or distance. Unlike a road race every finisher in a time trial receives a time and position in the field. In an 'open' event there are usually awards made to winners in numerous age-related categories.

It isn't necessary to ride a specialist low-profile time-trial machine, or wear a skinsuit or other aerodynamic aids, but there's no doubt that a combination of some or all of these things will help to maximise your efforts against the watch.

➔ **Time trialling is popular in the UK, with club and 'open' events on weekday evenings and weekends between spring and autumn.**

# Kit bag

Months of training can go to waste if you forget an important item of kit on the day of the event. Disasters ranging from arriving too late to forgetting your shoes or drinking bottles aren't unusual and most cyclists have learned the hard way that the only answer is to have a methodical and structured race-day plan.

Apart from your kit bag it's worth taking a track or stirrup

⬇ **A kit bag should contain extra clothing for rain or cold conditions.**

pump to ensure you have the correct tyre pressures before the start of the event. It's fine to travel to an event in your cycling kit as that's one less thing to worry about.

## Recommended kit bag contents
- Helmet and shoes.
- Towel and change of clothes.
- Spare inner tubes and tyre levers.
- Spare tyre.
- Basic toolkit or multi-tool.
- Long-sleeve jersey or jacket.
- Gilet top.
- Soft shell raincoat.
- Cycling mitts and full-length gloves.
- Arm and leg warmers.
- Cycling sunglasses.
- Overshoes for cold or rain.
- Filled bottles for the ride and after.
- Bottled water.
- Energy bars and gels.
- Sunblock.

# CHAPTER 8
# MAINTENANCE AND REPAIRS

**Modern bicycles are better made and more reliable than ever before, but a bicycle isn't a car, which can be driven day after day without so much as a drop of oil or a glance under the bonnet or at the tyres. If you don't wash a car for months it'll look uncared for but will still run perfectly well. Neglect a bike in the same way and premature wear will set in on some of the most expensive components. After a year you could be in for a big bill to replace the drivetrain.**

Bikes look fragile but can support a hefty fellow pounding the cranks for hours on end, over all sorts of roads. A bike can take a lot of abuse before it cries 'Enough!', and can even be ridden when parts are very worn or even broken. Just keeping a bike clean and lubricated will extend the life of its delicate components by years. Keeping them adjusted and replacing service parts will ensure the bike performs as well as it did when new.

In this chapter we'll show you how to maintain your bike on a daily basis as well as how to adjust and replace service parts. Cleaning, lubricating and working on your bike shouldn't be an occasional activity. It must be something you consider every time you ride your bike; even if you do nothing, checking a few basics like the chain and tyres are as important as any of your riding preparations.

← **Checking and maintaining your bike should be part of your regular cycling routine.**

# Bike cleaning

A clean bike will reward you with a quiet and trouble-free ride. The upshot of having a clean bike is the reduction in cost of

## Tools for the job

- General-purpose bike cleaner
- Drivetrain degreaser
- Water dispersant spray
- Chain lube, wet or dry
- Bucket
- Sponge
- Brushes
- Clean rags

**NON ESSENTIAL BUT USEFUL**
- Hose/jet wash
- Chain cleaning device
- Bike polish
- Bike work stand

replacing parts – clean bikes last longer. Regularly cleaning your bike allows you to get hands-on with its unique aspects and you soon become attuned to its character and construction, its many moving parts and even the components that don't move.

Here's a cleaning regime that'll get your bike into tip-top condition in less than 20 minutes.

With the bike set up on a work stand or leaning against a wall spray it all over with bike cleaner, paying particular attention to any really grimy areas such as behind the brake calipers, under the fork crown and under the bottom bracket area. Leave to soak for a few minutes.

### ➜ Degreasing

Using the degreaser, spray directly on to the chain (back pedalling to make sure all of the links are covered); other areas on which to use degreaser will be anything that the chain touches, like chainrings and chainset, front and rear derailleurs and cassette. A small paintbrush with the bristles cut down is handy for working degreaser into the chain, sprocket gaps and chainrings. Leave for a few minutes to let the degreaser break down the oil.

## Hard deposits

The jockey wheels can collect hard deposits of chain oil. Make sure you get rid of this (use a screwdriver tip or stiff brush) or it'll smear straight back on your nice shiny chain. If you use a chain cleaning device make sure you clean it once in a while, as the brushes get coated in old oil and debris and can make your chain worse!

### ➔ Get scrubbing!

If you've neglected your bike you might need to use brushes to loosen the caked-on dirt. You can buy bike-cleaning brushes to clean certain parts of your bike or just use 'normal' brushes, making sure that they're not going to damage the carbon. Normally a well-soaked sponge will shift dirt from the frame. Make sure you clean your wheel rims and the brake pads themselves of old brake residue.

### ➔ Rinse and repeat

Starting from the top parts of the bike (saddle, handlebars and top tube), use clean warm water and a sponge to rinse off the dirt and cleaning products. Don't neglect hidden areas under the saddle and bottom bracket, the chainstays and all around the fork blades.

### ➔ Drying

If it's warm and sunny give the bike a few minutes to dry off. Use a clean, absorbent cloth to dry the bike in the following order, using a separate cloth for the drivetrain:

Handlebars and shifters.
Saddle and seatpost.
Main frame.
Wheels and brakes.
Drivetrain.

### ➜ Water dispersant/light lube

Using a bike finisher or light lube or equivalent, spray a fine mist over the frame and most moving parts, back-pedalling to make sure the chain is coated. This will disperse any pooled water and prevent surface corrosion or blemishes that often appear the day after you've 'cleaned' your bike. Use the long nozzle to aim at inaccessible parts of the derailleurs, shifters and brake calipers that need lubricating. *Don't* spray on to wheel rims or brake pads – use a clean rag to shield these areas if you're spraying near them.

Leave for a few minutes and then use a clean cloth to wipe off any excess, finishing off with the chain by holding the cloth around the chain and running it through your hand while turning the pedals.

### ➜ Polish (optional)

For that real showroom finish and to add another layer of protection you can now apply a fine coat of bike polish to the main frame before buffing to a shine with another clean cloth. This will not only make your frame look new, but sticky dirt and road debris will find it harder to stick to it. Make sure polish isn't sprayed anywhere near braking surfaces.

### ➜ Chain lubrication

Now your bike is clean and shiny the last step is to lubricate the chain. For most of the year a 'dry' chain lube is best for road bikes. This tends not to pick up too much dirt from the road and is less likely to fly off. The only downside of dry lube is that it has to be reapplied after a couple of rides. For winter riding in harsher conditions switch to 'wet' lube, which lasts longer and doesn't get washed off but does pick up a lot of dirt and gets the classic black, oily look pretty quickly, which spreads everywhere.

If applying from a bottle, you only need a small amount applied to the inside of the rollers of each chain link, so don't drown your chain. Place the nozzle above the lower part of the chain and let the lube dribble on to the chain as you back-pedal through one complete revolution of the chain. Leave for ten minutes and then wipe off any excess. Ideally oil the chain the night before your ride.

If applying from an aerosol use the long thin nozzle a few millimetres from the chain rollers as you rotate the chain through one revolution.

**You only need to oil each roller once and if you have a split link that's a good place to start and finish. Alternatively mark the link where you start by giving it a little rub with a rag.**

# Changing an inner tube

Punctures are the great leveller of cyclists. Everyone from Chris Froome to a first-time rider has suffered the misery of a deflating tyre. Unlike Chris Froome and his compatriots in the pro peloton, however, most of us don't have a fully stocked support car at our beck and call on every ride, so being able to change a tube is a skill everyone needs to master.

Always carry a new inner tube when out riding, as trying to repair a puncture when it's cold and wet is time-consuming and miserable. It's best to bring the old tube home and put it with the rest to be repaired in front of the fire on a cold winter's night!

## Repair kit

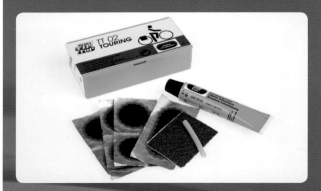

It can be worth carrying a puncture repair outfit or 'magic' patches if you're on a touring holiday or there's a chance you may run out of spare tubes. Another useful addition to a repair kit is a tyre 'boot', which is a roughly inch-square piece of old tyre sidewall or toothpaste tube that can be used to prevent the inner tube poking through a gash in the side of the tyre. This boot is placed on the inside of the gash and held in place by the inflated inner tube.

## Tools for the job

- Spare inner tube of correct size and valve length.
- Pump or CO2 inflator.
- Tyre levers.

➜ **Remove the wheel from the bike**

With the wheel in front of you, 'break the bead' of the tyre by pushing the side of the tyre inwards towards the centre of the rim. Do this all away around the wheel and on both sides – this'll make the tyre easier to take off.

Put the wheel vertically on the ground with the valve at the bottom. Starting on the top of the wheel opposite the valve, either lift the side of the tyre up and over the rim if the tyre is quite loose *or* insert the thin part of a tyre lever under the tyre bead to hook and lift the bead of the tyre over the rim.

If the tyre is very tight, insert another tyre lever approximately 150mm (6in) along from the first lever and lift both together to bring a larger area of bead over the rim.

If the tyre is loose use your hand to lift the rest of the tyre bead over the rim *or*, holding one tyre lever steady, slide the other around the rim to lift the bead over.

### Hook on lever

**Many tyre levers have a small hook at one end that you can place around a spoke to hold the tyre lever in place while you slide the other end round.**

Undo the valve lock-ring on the outside of the rim and pull the inner tube out of the tyre completely.

Lift off the other side of the tyre and remove the tyre from the wheel (you might need to use tyre levers).

Inspect the tyre for any sharp objects or large cuts by running a finger carefully around the whole of the inside of the tyre. Remove any debris. If there are any large cuts in the tyre the new inner tube might be forced through, so be sure to stick a tyre boot or self-adhesive patch to the inside to prevent further punctures. If it's too big, you might require a new tyre.

**7**

Put one side of the tyre back on the rim.

**8**

Inflate the new inner tube a small amount to give it some shape, put the valve back through the rim, thread the lock-ring on loosely and start pushing the tube into the tyre.

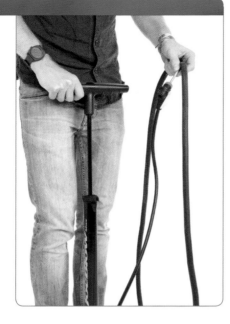

**9**

Starting at the valve, push the open side of the tyre back into the rim and, using both hands, feed the rest of the tyre back into place. It'll get harder towards the end. If you need to, carefully insert a tyre lever (try not to catch the tube with the tip) and very gently pop the remaining tyre bead into place. On an older tyre it may be possible to use your thumbs to finish off the job.

**10**

As you push the tyre bead into the centre of the rim check that no inner tube is stuck under the bead. If it is, it *will* pinch the inner tube and go bang as soon as you inflate!

**11**

Attach your preferred inflation device and pump a small amount of air into the tyre, checking the tyre bead is correctly seated and hasn't lifted off anywhere.

**12**

If everything is seated correctly, inflate to your preferred pressure (normally between 80–120psi depending on tyre width, weather conditions and rider weight).

**13**

Put wheel back on and continue your ride.

# The chain

Many riders don't realise that the forces put through a chain with every pedal stroke will in time wear and cause the chain to stretch. When a chain stretches it changes the way it interacts with the chainrings and cassette. Over time this chain wear

(sometimes called 'chain growth') will damage the aluminium teeth of the chainrings and the cassette sprockets so much that they fail to engage the chain, resulting, in the most extreme case, in the chain skipping or jumping on the gears.

If you let the wear get this far, just putting a new chain on won't solve the problem – you're probably looking at having to replace not only the chain but the chainrings and cassette too.

Checking for chain wear regularly and replacing your chain as soon as it's reached its serviceable limits will greatly extend the life of your drivetrain as well as ensure that the transmission runs smoothly and quietly.

 **Tools for the job**

- Chain splitter (either individual or part of a multi-tool).
- Chain-wear checking device.
- Spare 'quick link' or matching chain links and pins.

To check your chain for wear, use a chain checker. These come in a variety of styles but most push into the top of the chain and will indicate if it's still within its service limits. If the chain checker indicates that it's time to replace the chain the first thing to do is remove the old chain.

If your old chain has a quick link, you can squeeze it apart, which is most easily done with a quick link removal tool but it can also be unclipped by adept use of a flat-bladed tool.

**3**

If the chain doesn't have a quick link, use a chain splitter to push the old joining pin out. Carefully extract the old chain from the derailleurs, making a mental note of how it goes through them. Don't throw it away just yet.

**4**

Make sure the derailleurs are in the highest gears (big ring at the front, smallest cog at the back). Carefully guide the new chain through the derailleurs – put one end of the chain through the front derailleur and over the chainring and thread the other end over the cassette and through the rear derailleur so the ends dangle down.

**5**

With the chain on the big chainring and in the smallest cog of the cassette, hold on to both ends of the chain and bring them together. As the ends of the chain start overlapping look at the jockey wheels on the rear derailleur. When they hang directly below each other (with the bike level) the chain is at the correct length.

**6**

Remove any superfluous links, leaving the male/ female links at the end of the chain depending on how you're going to join it (two inner links if using a quick link, or one outer and one inner if using a joining pin). Using a chain hook to hold the chain tight will free up both hands to link the chain with much less hassle. You can make a chain hook out of a broken spoke.

**7**

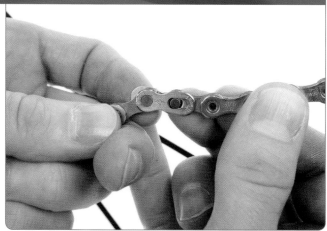

If using a quick link, join the two ends of the chain by inserting the plate with both pins facing towards you ready to accept the linking side plate. Push the side plate on to the exposed ends of the pins.

**8**

Rotate the chain so the quick link is above the chainring, and while holding the back wheel apply forward pressure to the pedal to 'click' the link into place.

**9**

If using a joining pin, push the pin through the two ends of chain. Wind out the chain tool and put the chain link with the protruding pin into the furthest position.

**10**

Wind the chain tool in until the pin is flush with the outer plate – look at the other links to gauge how much should be showing. When happy, snap off the pointed end of the pin to leave it looking 'normal'.

**11**

Sometimes this link can be quite stiff and you might need to flex it very carefully sideways to free it up. Or you can place the 'stiff' link in the middle slot on the chain tool and apply a very small amount of pressure to one side of the joining pin to release the link.

## Chain length

**The simplest way to work out the correct length of a replacement chain is to lay it next to the old one and remove enough links to get the correct length.**

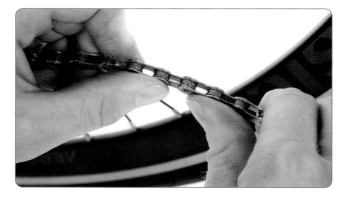

# Rear derailleur

For many people the intricate workings of a derailleur, with its odd screws, adjusters and moving parts, are something that's best left to a mechanic. Many's the time a poor customer has come into a bike shop with a wild look in their eyes saying they've tried 'everything' to get their gears working to no avail. This invariably means that screws and other adjusters have been turned with no thought as to the consequences, and soon the derailleur has no hope of working as it should!

This guide should help to simplify the procedure of setting up a rear derailleur from new or adjusting an existing one.

## 🔧 Tools for the job

- **Small flat-head or cross-head screwdriver.**
- **Pliers.**
- **Bike stand.**

## Standard derailleur

The standard rear derailleur has four ways in which it can be adjusted. Understanding this is key to knowing what to touch and, more importantly, what to leave alone.

### 1 Barrel adjuster

This is the most important part for adjusting gear selection as it alters the cable tension. It's situated just behind where the cable is clamped to the derailleur. Turning it will move the derailleur up a gear or down a gear.

### 2 'High' and 'low' limit screws

These stop the derailleur shifting too far, preventing the chain from being jammed into the frame or dropping into the spokes of the wheel. They're often stamped 'H' (high) and 'L' (low).

### 3 B-tension adjustment screw

This screw alters the distance of the top jockey wheel in relation to the cassette.

## Jockey wheels

Jockey wheels are the two small, toothed cogs that guide the chain through the derailleur and on to the cassette, sometimes called guide pulleys. They sit between two plates called the cage, which hangs below the derailleur body.

### Bent derailleur hanger

There are three common reasons for rear shift problems: a bent derailleur hanger; incorrect gear cable tension; or worn chain and/or cassette. If when you shift gear it jumps two sprockets at a time or doesn't go up or down the cassette smoothly, you might have a bent derailleur hanger. This is the piece of aluminium or steel that your derailleur bolts on to and which in turn bolts on to your frame dropout (in most cases). It's designed to bend or snap before damaging your expensive frame or derailleur. A knock or crash, weight pressing on the derailleur or even frequent shifting under load can all cause the hanger to bend.

If you stand directly behind the bike looking at the derailleur, the jockey wheels should be vertically aligned and run directly in line with the cassette. If they look bent or twisted, even by a tiny amount, then you might need to have the hanger realigned. This is a job for your local bike shop. They'll be able to use a specific tool to realign the hanger. If it's badly bent you'll need to replace it with a new one. Hangers are specific to the make and model of frame and are inexpensive to buy.

### Worn chain or cassette

If your gears are jumping or skipping when you apply power then your chain and cassette might be badly worn. This can be checked quite easily using a chain checker. Chains stretch over time and can get to a point where they start wearing the teeth of the cassette and chainrings until the gears fail to engage properly. The only solution is a new chain and cassette, and quite possibly chainrings too.

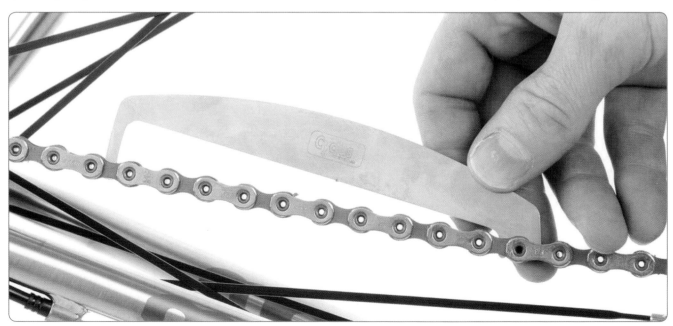

## Adjusting the rear derailleur

**1** With the chain on the small chainring, change gear until it's on the smallest sprocket.

**2** If when changing up through the cassette you notice any hesitations or the chain fails to sit on the sprocket properly, your cable tension might be too slack. Using the barrel adjuster on the back of the derailleur (or on the frame or cable) unwind it anticlockwise half a turn at a time to tension the cable until the chain shifts smoothly and quickly on to each cog.

**3** Shift back down to make sure you haven't tightened the cable too much. If you have, wind in the barrel adjuster clockwise a small amount until you reach a good compromise between up shifts and down shifts.

## Resetting the derailleur cable

**1** If the barrel adjuster doesn't have enough range of adjustment along its threaded length you'll need to tension the cable at the anchor bolt. Put the derailleur back in the smallest sprocket (lowest cable tension) then loosen the anchor bolt until the cable can move freely.

**2** Before taking the slack out of the cable, reset the barrel adjuster to approximately halfway.

**3** Gripping the end of the cable with pliers, pull it through the anchor bolt until it feels taut along its length. Tighten the anchor bolt securely.

## Adjustment of the B-tension screw

This is normally only necessary if you've changed to a cassette with bigger sprockets.

**1** If the top jockey wheel rubs against the largest cog of the cassette the B-tension screw can be tightened to move the derailleur away from the cassette.

**2** Keep the pedals turning as you're adjusting the screw, as the largest sprocket only just needs to clear the top jockey

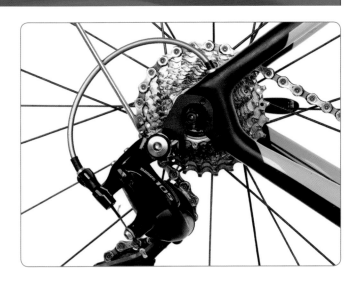

## Limit screw adjustments

As you shift to the far ends of the cassette the limit screws on the derailleur will stop the chain from going into the wheel (the L limit screw) or jamming in the frame (the H limit screw). If the chain or derailleur cage goes into the spokes, it can quickly escalate into a catastrophic event, ripping the derailleur from the frame and potentially causing a crash as the damaged wheel tangles with the gears.

**1** Ideally with the bike in a stand, set the high and low limits with the chain on the smallest (H) and biggest (L) sprockets. If the gear runs smoothly turn the screw until it starts to 'clack' then back it off.

**2** On the low setting, turn the pedals very slowly and check by eye that the derailleur cage is a few millimetres from the spokes.

**3** Turn the L screw until you can just see the cage moving away from the spokes then back it off.

# Adjusting the front derailleur

The front derailleur has a tough job – it has to force its thin metal or carbon plates to push a chain under massive tension from one chainring to another. The fact it does this without much fuss and usually without lots of rattles and noise is nothing short of an engineering wonder. A well-adjusted front mech should give years of good service.

### Tools for the job

■ 4mm and 5mm hex keys.
■ Small flat-head or cross-head screwdriver.
■ Bike stand.

**1**

If the front derailleur isn't shifting smoothly, is dragging on the chain or simply not shifting out of one chainring to another, the alignment needs checking. Shift gear to put the chain on to the small ring (this reduces cable tension, making it easier to make adjustments). Looking from above, the derailleur cages should run parallel with the chainrings. If this isn't the case, loosen the mounting bolt for the derailleur gently, manually move the cages until they line up with the chainrings then tighten the bolt firmly.

**2**

Shift into the big ring – check vertical alignment by looking side-on at the bottom of the outside cage of the derailleur. This should be approximately 3mm above the top of the chainring teeth. If it needs adjusting, shift back into the small ring, loosen the mounting bolt again and move up or down the correct amount (making sure the cages are still parallel with the chainrings).

**3**

Because of the forces used to shift the chain on to a larger chainring the cable can stretch and cable tension reduce, preventing shifts on to the big ring. If your bike has an inline barrel adjuster installed in the cable or on the frame stop, you can try winding it out to see if there is enough movement to compensate for the slack in the cable.

**4**

If there are no barrel adjusters, shift the chain and derailleur on to the big ring (you might need to do it manually); then, without turning the pedals, shift the derailleur on to the small ring. This will release tension in the cable without having to fight against the derailleur.

**5**

Loosen the cable pinch bolt and pull through a small amount of cable (1–3mm) then re-tighten the bolt. Turn the pedals to check it goes into the small ring then shift back into the big ring, checking it goes in smoothly. Repeat if more cable tension is needed.

**Alternative approach:** Wind in the 'L' limit screw to prevent the derailleur from dropping down before shifting into the smallest gear to adjust cable tension. Make sure to wind the screw back out again before checking shifting!

**6**

Sometimes the derailleur can drop the chain off the small ring and into the frame, or overshift, pushing the chain off the big ring and down on to the crank arm. This can be prevented by adjusting the high and low limit screws. Fortunately most are quite sensibly positioned, with the screw adjusting low shifts (into the frame) next to the frame or labelled 'L' (low) and high shifts (off towards the crank arm) nearest the outside stamped 'H' (high). Screwing them into the derailleur will restrict the movement of the derailleur in that direction.

Sometimes the limit screws need to be wound out to prevent rubbing of the chain on the derailleur cage. Make sure you're spinning the cranks when adjusting the screws either way to prevent overcorrection.

Clean out the heads to the screws thoroughly and use a good screwdriver (flat-head is normally my preferred choice) as they can round off easily.

# Handlebar tape

Some types of bar tape are easier to wrap than others, so if you're relatively inexperienced, it's worth using a 'cork' type or thinner rubbery tape as these stretch quite well to allow easier wrapping and a smoother finish. A lot of tape has a sticky backing which can be left on if you need to have a practice wrap before removing the backing tape and doing it for real.

**Tools for the job**
- New bar tape.
- Electrical/insulating tape.
- Sharp scissors.
- Bike stand or some form of bike support.

Remove the old bar tape and pick off any residue. Peel back the shifter hoods.

Unravel the new bar tape and peel off a good length of the backing tape. Stick the electrical tape to the top tube of the bike within easy reach and keep the scissors to hand.

Starting at the end of the handlebar, place one end of the tape underneath and facing towards the outside of the bike. Make sure there's an overlap of about half the tape's width at the end of the bar (this is to tuck in at the end).

Holding the tape in place with your other hand, start wrapping over the top of the bar towards the outside at a slight forward angle. Only overlap about a quarter to one-third the width of the previous wrap. Pull the tape nice and tight until you've fully enclosed the end of the bar with the correct overlap.

Continue to spiral the tape around the bar, maintaining the same tension on the tape. Slightly twisting the top part of the tape towards the bar will keep it tight and prevent it from ballooning outwards creating ridges or gaps as you get to the tricky bend in the bar.

As you get close to the shifter you'll need to wrap the tape in a figure-of-eight shape from underneath the shifter to over the top and back again. The critical factor is not to leave any gaps in the tape when the lever hood is put back in place. Try to angle the tape to cover the shifter attachment band (normally shiny silver) – this will ensure you've left no gaps.

**Alternative approach:** A lot of handlebar tape comes with two small pieces of tape that can be used to wrap the shifter bracket. If these are used, it'll make wrapping the tape round the shifters easier, just a little more bulky.

When you reach the top of the bars you'll need to wrap around the bend, so adopt the same principle as for the bottom part, maintaining tension on the tape and keeping the overlap the same.

As you reach the point where you'd like to end the tape check the whole length for any errors, such as gaps or poor overlaps, and when you're satisfied cut the tape at an angle to produce a nice straight finish – don't let go of the end at this point or all your good work will unravel!

Hold the end of the tape in place and wrap electrical tape to secure the bar tape to the handlebar. Try to keep the electrical tape nice and tight and in a neat straight line. Cut so it finishes under the bar.

Push the ends of the tape into the bar and secure in place using the end plug provided or one of your own choice – you might need to gently tap it in place or secure it using Allen keys in this case, tucking in any wayward edges as you finish.

Repeat steps 3–9 on the other side. Try to replicate the same number of wraps above and below the shifter and end the tape the same distance from the stem as before.

# Headset

Riding your bike with a loose headset (or even one that's too tight) can result in damage to the bearings and ultimately could lead to irreparable damage to the frame or the forks or, in very extreme cases, catastrophic failure. But that's a worst-case scenario, and as long you maintain your headset and keep it correctly adjusted, it should give years of reliable service.

## Tools for the job

- 4mm, 5mm, 6mm hex keys (specific headsets/ stems might need Torx or other sizes).
- Plastic/rubber/wooden mallet.
- Teflon grease.
- Cleaning rags.
- Degrease spray.
- Headset check and adjustment.

To check if your headset needs adjusting or the bearings need servicing or replacing, first turn your handlebars from side to side. Does the movement feel rough or stiff? If so, your headset will need to be stripped. If the bearings feel smooth it's time to check the headset adjustment.

While holding the front brake on, rock the bike backward and forward. If there's a 'knocking' feeling through the bars your headset might be loose. To make sure it's the headset, wrap your hand around the top of the fork and the bottom of the head tube and rock it again – you'll feel movement between the two if it's the headset.

Loosen the two stem bolts. The stem clamps the bearings in place and no adjustment is possible until it's freed off.

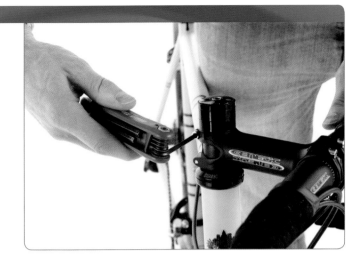

Gently tighten the top cap bolt until there's no more play in the headset. Check by rocking the bike. Stop when there's no noticeable play or knocking. Turn the bars. If the steering feels stiff you've tightened the top cap too much. Undo the top cap bolt until the steering feels smooth without any play.

When you're happy with the adjustment, position the stem back in line with the front wheel and tighten the stem bolts equally to lock the headset in place. When tightening stem bolts, tighten each one alternately – this will maintain even clamping tension on the steerer.

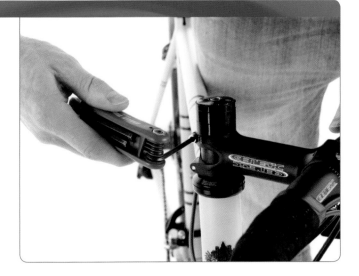

## Dismantling the headset

 **4**

To replace the headset bearings, first of all remove the top cap, bolt and any spacers above the stem completely.

 **5**

Loosen the stem bolts and carefully remove the stem, as the forks might drop through the frame. Hold on to the forks to stop them sliding out of the frame. Let the handlebars gently rest next to the frame. It's worth removing the front wheel to reduce the chances of the fork dropping out too quickly.

 **6**

Remove any spacers under the stem (make a note of how many were under/over the stem) and the headset/bearing cover and any thin washers on top of the bearing.

 **7**

There's a wedge-shaped spacer called a compression ring holding everything together that might stop the fork from dropping down through the frame. If it's very tight, take a wooden or plastic mallet and tap the top of the forks to release it. Slide the compression ring and any seals off the steerer tube and slide the forks out of the frame.

Remove the bearings from the frame – there should be one at the top and another at the bottom of the head tube (the bottom one might be on the fork crown). Clean old grease and dirt out of the frame and bearing seats using rags and a light spray of degreaser.

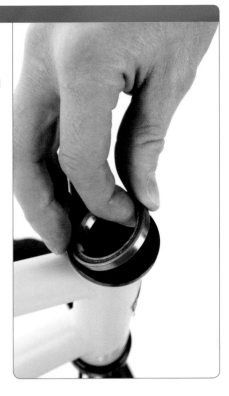

Wipe the bearings clean – don't use degreaser. If they feel smooth and in good condition retain them. If you're replacing the bearings, make sure you replace with exactly the same.

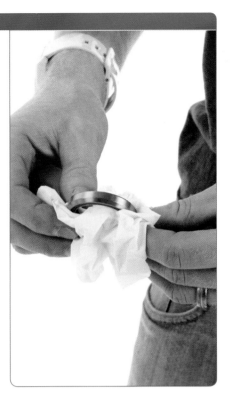

## Replacing bearings

Apply clean grease liberally to the bearing seats in the frame and fit/refit the bearings in the same position – normally with the chamfered edge facing into the frame. Bearings come in a range of sizes; normally the part number is etched into the side. Take the bearing to a bike shop if you're unsure.

Smear grease on top of the bearings; this will help prevent water and other contaminants from getting past the seals. Refit the headset parts in the correct order – compression ring and seal, bearing cover, headset spacers, stem, headset spacers (if any) and top cap and bolt. Follow instructions for adjustment (see above) and wipe off any excess grease.

# Brakes

The traditional caliper brake is relatively simple with few moving parts and is easy to maintain. Service parts are cables and brake pads, both of which can last years if looked after and used in dry conditions. Setting up the brakes for optimal performance and individual preferences is the most important job for the home mechanic.

### Tools for the job

- **Hex keys (normally 5mm, 4mm and possibly a 2mm or 2.5mm).**
- **Torx keys (for some calipers).**
- **Small flat-head or cross-head screwdriver.**

Give the brake lever a squeeze to identify any issues. Things you're looking for could be the lever pulling back too far, a rough lever feel (dirty or worn cable), a sticky caliper (not releasing) and pad wear.

If the brake lever's pulling back too far and not allowing you to apply full power, the brake blocks might be worn or the cable might have stretched. If the brake blocks are still serviceable, the caliper arms can be adjusted to sit closer to the rim. On the top of the caliper arm where the cable goes in there's normally a barrel adjuster that can be wound in to 'close' the caliper by a millimetre or two. Slacken off the lock nut and wind in the barrel adjuster a quarter turn at a time.

If the caliper's still sitting too far off the rim the cable can be undone and pulled through the clamp. Pull the caliper together with your hand, bringing the pads into contact with the rim. That will de-tension the cable, allowing adjustment without the caliper springing open. Make sure the quick release isn't off or open and screw out the barrel adjuster until three-quarters of the thread is showing. With the brake squeezed, loosen the cable pinch bolt with a 5mm hex key until the cable is free to move.

Allow the cable to move through the clamp while holding the brake blocks very close to the rim. Tighten the cable pinch bolt securely and pull the brake lever to check if it feels right. If the blocks are too close to the rim, screwing in the barrel adjuster a couple of turns may back off the brake just enough.

## Replacing brake pads

If brake pads are worn out, they sit too far off the rim, can lose some 'feel' and power and should be replaced before they damage the rims. Most modern brake pads come in two parts, the brake pad or insert and a metal holder or cartridge. If your pads are the older one-piece design, you might want to upgrade now, as one of the benefits of a quality set of modern pads is better braking performance.

With the wheel removed, undo the grub screw on the end of the brake pad holder, being careful not to lose it.

Slide the old pad out towards the opening at the back end of the holder and discard. You might need to carefully use a thin screwdriver to lever the pad out.

Slide a new pad in. A little dab of chain lube on the edges of the pad holder will help slide the new pad into place.

They're normally marked on the back 'R' (right), 'L' (left) and 'Forward'. It also helps to note how the old pads where marked and placed.

Nip up the grub screw. It locks the pad in place but shouldn't be overtight. If you'd previously adjusted the brake cable to take up the slack from worn pads, you might need to release some of the tension, as the new pads will sit much closer to the rim.

## Aligning brake pads

Check the alignment of the brake pads against the rim by pulling the brake lever until the pads are pressed up against the rim. Looking closely at the pad, check that it's in contact with the braking surface only, not touching the tyre or dropping below the trailing edge.

If you need to adjust the pad, slacken off the 4mm hex bolt holding the pad/holder to the caliper while applying the brake (this prevents the pad from dropping off the rim).

Move the pad into the correct position and then tighten the hex bolt, making sure you check the pad stays in position against the twisting of the bolt. Release the brake and pull again to check the alignment.

To prevent brake squeal you might need to 'toe in' the pad. This means angling the pad so that the leading edge hits the rim slightly before the rear. A quality brake pad sits on a dished washer that allows enough micro-adjustment to toe in the front of the pad.

## Aligning the caliper

Sometimes one pad makes contact with the rim before the other, pushing the wheel to one side when braking. To align the caliper, insert a 5mm hex key into the caliper mounting bolt – behind the fork crown for the front brake or behind the seatstay bridge for the rear.

Loosen it a small amount until the caliper can move freely, then apply and hold the brake.

With the brake held on, tighten the bolt and check the alignment. If it's still a little out use your hand to manually adjust until both pads touch the rim at the same time.

# Hydraulic disc brakes

Despite featuring on mountain bikes for many years, disc brakes on road bikes are still a relatively novel phenomenon, and have proved controversial for racing. There are arguments for and against disc brakes, but one that should appeal to the home mechanic is the potential reduction in maintenance over a typical rim brake.

### Tools for the job

- Hex keys (2–6mm).
- Torx keys (T25, T30).
- Clean, flat-bladed screwdriver (wide tip).
- Sandpaper (medium grit).
- Needle-nose pliers.
- Disc brake cleaner.
- Clean rag.

## General disc brake check

Spin the wheel. Do you hear any rubbing sounds? Look at the rotor from above while it's spinning and check it runs straight. If so, a simple realignment of the caliper may be all that's required.

Undo the two bolts holding the caliper to the frame/fork leg just enough to let the caliper move freely.

Spin the wheel and pull the brake lever.

With the brake lever held tightly on, tighten the two caliper bolts. Let go of the brake lever and spin the wheel. The rotor should now sit centrally in the caliper without any rubbing. If you still notice any rubbing, the rotor might not be straight. It can be carefully straightened with a specialist tool but is probably best left to a bike shop.

Remove the wheel. With your clean, flat-bladed screwdriver, carefully push the pads and pistons back into each side of the caliper. As pads wear the brake pistons become more and more exposed. If you don't push the pistons back in before fitting new pads, the rotor won't have enough space to spin freely.

With the bike on the ground, pull on the brake lever. Does it come back very close to the handlebar but still brake with power? In this case the pads will need inspecting and possibly replacing.

**7**

Remove the brake pads by carefully pulling out the retaining pins holding them in place. Extract both pads together.

**8**

If the pads have plenty of wear left but are glazed (shiny), use sandpaper to roughen the surfaces again. They should then work properly when refitted (after bedding in). However, pads can become contaminated by oils and lubricating sprays, so if they continue not to work or look to be coated in contaminants, they'll need to be replaced.

**9**

Reverse the steps for fitting new pads. Make sure to have any separating springs correctly fitted between the pads. Refit the wheel and check the alignment. You might need to realign the caliper to finish. If the brake squeals, a small amount of copperslip applied to the back of each brake pad – not the braking surface – can help reduce the noise.

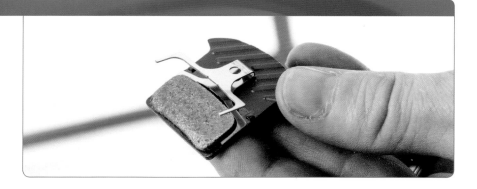

## 'Bedding in'

**New pads require bedding in. Treat your rotors with a flash cleaner to get rid of any contaminants first. Find a safe place and do several quick runs while dragging both brakes for a few seconds at a time, making sure to increase braking pressure until you stop. The brake should feel more powerful with each run.**

# Bottom bracket

**Tools for the job**

- Hex keys: 5mm (6–8mm for pedals).
- External BB socket tool/ spanner (different BB brands might need different tools).
- Socket tool.
- Preload cap tool (Shimano).
- Torque wrench (ideally).
- Flat-bladed screwdriver.
- Plastic or wooden mallet.
- Spray degreaser.
- Grease.
- Clean rags.

The bottom bracket (BB) is the set of bearings upon which the cranks spin. It takes the most punishment of any component on your bike so wear rates can be frightening – especially if you ride in all weathers. Unfortunately most bottom brackets are sealed units, which means that once they're showing signs of wear it's out with the old, in with the new.

## Checking threaded bottom bracket

Eliminate the pedals as the cause of the noise. Remove and check them for rough bearings or excessive play. Try another set of pedals if you're not sure.

Once the pedals are ruled out, hold on to the crank arms and rock them sideways to look for obvious play in the bottom bracket bearings. If there is play, the bearings need to be replaced.

**③**

To get to the bottom bracket you'll need to remove the chainset. With Shimano systems firstly loosen the two 5mm bolts on the left-hand crank.

**④**

Use the preload cap tool to remove the plastic preload cap.

**⑤**

With the flat-bladed screwdriver, push up the retaining clip before removing the left-hand crank arm. You should then be able to push the axle through the BB to remove the chainset fully. If it doesn't want to move, use the mallet to tap the axle through gently. Don't forget to take the chain off the chainring when removing the chainset.

The BB cups are threaded differently – the non-drive-side cup uses a standard thread, but the drive-side cup uses a left-hand thread, which undoes clockwise. If you seat the tool pointing towards the front of the bike and push down this unscrews the cups on either side. The BB should be tight, so you might need a tool with a long handle or an extension bar to generate enough leverage.

Clean out the bottom bracket shell thoroughly with degreaser and clean rags. Inspect the frame thread for any damage before applying new, clean grease.

Carefully thread the right-hand cup into the frame, making sure not to cross-thread it. Tighten clockwise, pushing towards the back of the bike, to the recommended torque (normally very tight). Then fit the left-hand cup in the same way.

Refit the chainset. You can apply a thin layer of grease to the axle. Tighten the preload cap hand-tight until there's no play. Push the retaining clip down and finally tighten the two bolts to the recommended torque.

# Wheel repairs

The following steps focus on simple techniques to get your wheel useable either when out on a ride or as a simple home fix. As with any technical repair, if in doubt, take your wheel to your local bike shop as they'll have experts on hand who can make sure your bike is safe to ride.

## Spoke tension

To be able to true and tension a wheel properly relies on an understanding of the relationship between the components of a wheel. Spokes are normally attached to the hub using a fixed end and then threaded into a spoke nipple held in place at the rim. Alternate spokes are attached to different sides of the rim and hub, so when the spoke nipple is tightened on to the spoke it pulls the rim over to whichever side of the hub the particular spoke is attached.

The wheel-builder's art is in creating perfect tension between both sides of spokes to allow the wheel to run both round and true, side-to-side and vertically.

## Tools for the job

■ Spoke key.
■ Spoke rule or tape measure.
■ Zip ties.
■ Tape.
■ Wheel jig (optional).

 Slowly spin the wheel and try to identify the area of the rim that's out of true. Stop the wheel at that point.

 Check the spokes in that area of the wheel for damage and to ensure they don't feel loose (ie, can be moved easier than the others). If the wheel pulls to the left check the spokes that attach on the right side of the hub.

 If any loose spokes are found, mark them with a little piece of tape to allow easy identification.

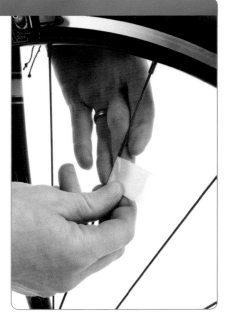

 Using a spoke key, tighten each nipple half a turn at a time (clockwise if looking down from the tyre-side of the wheel) until you see the wheel start to pull back into alignment. Often the spokes on either side of the loose spoke will need to be adjusted to compensate. Loosen the adjacent, opposite-side spoke by a quarter of a turn to make it more even.

Tighten the two spokes attached to the same side of the hub (either side of the loose spoke) by a small amount, normally a quarter turn at a time. But go easy on the spoke key – tightening too much will pull the wheel further out of true.

If you've found a broken spoke, it'll need replacing with a spoke of the exact same length and type. You can either measure the broken parts of the spoke, estimate the length of a spoke on the same side of the wheel using a tape measure or, as a last resort, remove another undamaged spoke. If measuring a spoke in situ, allow for the threaded length of the spoke hidden in the nipple (normally 8–10mm).

When fitting a new spoke take careful note of which side the spoke threads through the hub and how it crosses other spokes, and be sure to copy the position of other, similar spokes. Don't worry about flexing it, as it'll straighten under tension.

Insert the spoke nipple carefully into the rim – thread it slightly, upside down, on to the end of another spoke to hold it in place.

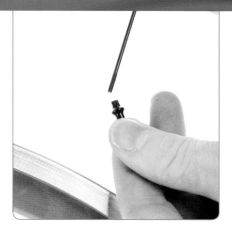

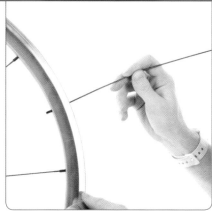

Locate the threaded end of the new spoke into the nipple and tighten it with your fingers. If you used another spoke to help installation, remove it. Tighten up and tension as explained above.

If you don't have a wheel-truing jig, you can attach zip ties to your fork/seat stays to use as indicators of any unwanted sideways movement – they can be moved closer as the wheel straightens.

# Worn cassette or chainrings

## Tools for the job

- Cassette removal tool (appropriate for make of cassette).
- Chain whip.
- Adjustable spanner (if needed).
- Hex keys (appropriate sizes for chainset/chainrings).
- Torx keys (optional, for some chainring removal).
- Crank installation tool (for Shimano chainsets).
- Chainring nut wrench.

If you're the sort of rider who replaces their chain regularly then you could enjoy years of service from your cassette and even longer from the chainrings. Inevitably, however, there'll eventually come a time when either component (or sometimes both) will need replacing.

## Checking the chainrings

 Check wear on existing chainrings. Teeth will start looking more like shark fins than a uniform shape as wear increases. If they're badly worn, it's time to replace them.

 Remove the chainset and take out the chainring bolts. Use the chainring nut wrench to hold the outer part of the bolt steady.

 Remove chainrings carefully from the crank arm.

 Fit new chainrings. The outer chainring has a small pin attached to prevent the chain from dropping on to the crank arm. Make sure it's fitted behind the crank arm. Loosely tighten the chainring bolts on alternate sides to even out the tension across the chainring. Only tighten the bolts to the recommended torque – aluminium bolts can be easily snapped.

Fully tighten bolts and replace chainset.

## Replacing the cassette

 **1**

To replace the cassette, first remove the rear wheel from the bike and remove the quick-release skewer.

 **2**

Insert cassette removal tool into the lockring – use an adjustable spanner to hold in place if needed.

 **3**

Wrap the chain from the chain whip around the cassette to stop the cassette spinning when pressure's applied to the removal tool.

 **4**

With the wheel in front of you and cassette facing outwards, push down on both tools to release the lock ring fully. Keep your hands widely spaced on the tools to avoid hitting the cassette.

 **5**

Remove the worn cassette. Wipe off any old grease/dirt. Inspect freehub body for signs of wear.

 **3**

Fit new cassette, making sure the splines line up. Attach lock ring and tighten fully. Replace skewer and refit wheel.

# Pre-event bike prep

Do these simple checks before most rides, certainly a few days before a big event just in case you spot something serious.

**1** Give the front wheel a spin. Check for damage and trueness of the rim. Make sure it doesn't rub on the brakes.

**2** The braking surface should be flat and not concave, which indicates a worn braking track.

**3** Have a look at the spokes and hub for damage. At the same time inspect both the brake pads for excess or unusual wear.

**4** Gripping the wheel, try and move it sideways in the fork. You're looking and feeling for play in the hub bearings. Check the quick-release is tightened correctly.

Now's a good time to feel for any damage or excessive wear to the tyres. Check the tyres for cuts and embedded flints and make sure the valves aren't bent.

Apply the front brake and rock the bike back and forth. You're feeling for any play in the headset bearings. You might want to place your other hand around the bearing and frame/fork to detect any unwanted movement.

Check the handlebar and stem bolts are correctly tightened and aligned.

**8**

Holding on to the crank, try to rock it sideways. Here we're looking for play in the bottom bracket bearings. Check the pedals and crank bolts are secure. While looking in this general area, check the front derailleur for damage and alignment.

**9**

While checking your pedals it might be a good time to also check the cleats on your shoes for wear.

**10**

Moving up to the saddle and seatpost. check that all the bolts are tight, the saddle points forward and that there's no damage to either.

Repeat the front-wheel checks for the rear wheel, making sure you also rock the cassette cogs to check for excess play.

While back-pedalling (spinning the cranks around backwards), check the chain for damage. Looking from behind the bike, check that the rear derailleur and hanger are aligned and that the jockey/pulley wheels are in good condition and tightly fastened.

Finally, check all other accessories are securely fastened, bottle cages and computer mounts especially.

BRINGING YOU THE
# BEST
## ROAD CYCLING
## CONTENT
*in*
## PRINT & ONLINE

PRINT **ON SALE EVERY THURSDAY** ▪ ONLINE **CYCLINGWEEKLY.CO.UK**

First published in 1891, the magazine has an amazing and unrivalled heritage, having been at the heart of British cycling for over 125 years.